Wild Birding Colorado

The Big Year of 2010

Cole Wild
Nicholas Komar

Outskirts Press, Inc.
Denver, Colorado

Wild Birding Colorado
The Big Year of 2010

Cover photo: White-tailed Ptarmigan at Rocky Mountain National Park.
Copyright © 2011 photos by Cole Wild
www.outskirtspress.com/wildbirdingcolorado

Outskirts Press, Inc.
http://www.outskirtspress.com

ISBN: 978-1-4327-7103-4

Library of Congress Control Number: 2011924067

Outskirts Press and the "OP" logo are trademarks belonging to Outskirts Press, Inc.

PRINTED IN THE UNITED STATES OF AMERICA

To our families, Bruce, Ava, and Cody Wild,
Elena Maribel, Angela Victoria, and
Nicholas Alexander Komar, and the birds.

Chapters

List of Photographic Figures

Collaborator's Preface

WILD BIRDING COLORADO IS AN account of a young naturalist who takes the competitive aspect of birding to a new level. In telling the story of Cole Wild's attempt to break the record for the number of bird species seen in a single year in Colorado, this book illuminates Wild's detour to birding greatness while searching for his ultimate niche in life. The book reveals the obsessiveness of birding and at the same time offers to both novice and expert naturalists a valuable trove of bird-lore and nature adventure.

As a friend of Cole Wild, and somewhat of an "extreme birder" myself, I followed Cole's Big Year attempt with great interest. When I realized the significance of his feats, I convinced him that this book needed to be written. Together we devised a plan to bring this project to fruition. With my writing experience (I have authored or co-authored more than 100 scientific journal articles), I would help bring his stories to life on the written page. The stories are his, not mine. As the writer, I functioned as his interpreter.

In writing the text I drew upon my own knowledge of Colorado's birds and birding in order to provide a context for Cole's experiences and to weave a more compelling story. Cole and I reviewed all of the material carefully to avoid printing incorrect information in the book.

My own insights into birds and birding in Colorado began to develop 38 years ago in Massachusetts when I became obsessed with competitive birding. I came to Colorado in May of 1997, and have kept an annual Year List of Colorado birds ever since.

Working with Cole on this project has been an exciting and satisfying endeavor. However, it was not without sacrifice, as any project of this magnitude requires an enormous investment of time and energy. In addition to the acknowledgments that Cole includes at the end of the book, I also wish to acknowledge the efforts of the staff at Outskirts Press, and more importantly, the support of my wife Maribel, and my children Angela and Nick, to whom I dedicate this book.

– Nicholas Komar
Fort Collins, Colorado

1. Antero Reservoir
2. Bonny Lake State Park
3. Boyd Lake State Park
4. Chatfield State Park
5. Cherry Creek State Park
6. Flagler State Wildlife Area
7. Fossil Creek Reservoir
8. Frenchman Creek State Wildlife Area
9. Horsetooth Reservoir
10. Jackson Lake State Park
11. John Martin Reservoir State Park
12. Jumbo Reservoir State Wildlife Area
13. MacFarlane Reservoir
14. Mesa Verde National Park
15. Monte Vista National Wildlife Refuge
16. NeeNoshe Reservoir

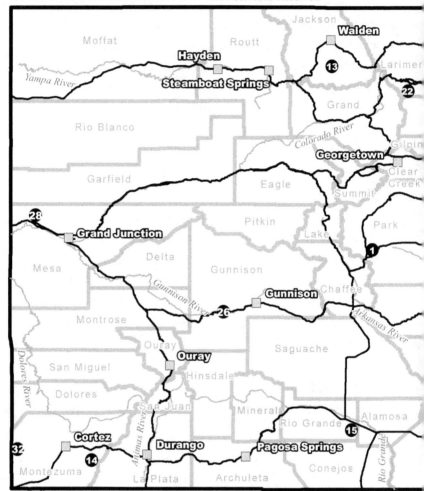

Colorado

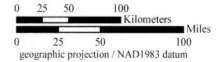

geographic projection / NAD1983 datum

17. Pawnee National Grassland
18. Prewitt Reservoir State Wildlife Area
19. Pueblo Reservoir State Park
20. Red Lion State Wildlife Area
21. Rocky Ford State Wildlife Area
22. Rocky Mountain National Park
23. Tamarack Ranch State Wildlife Area
24. Two Buttes State Wildlife Area

25. Black Hollow Reservoir
26. Blue Mesa Reservoir
27. Dixon Reservoir
28. Highline Lake
29. Lower Latham Reservoir
30. McIntosh Reservoir
31. Riverside Reservoir
32. Yellowjacket Canyon

Legend

⬜	City	〰️	Major River
❶⁷	Point of Interest	⬜	State Boundary
—	Major Highway	🔲	County Boundary

CHAPTER ONE

Prologue

I READ KENN KAUFMAN'S *KINGBIRD Highway* when I was twenty years old. As a teenager, Kenn was an oddball among American youth, more interested in observing and learning about our feathered companions on this Earth than the materialistic pursuits that pervade our Western society, such as the latest fashions and video games. Television and sports occupied a large chunk of my teenage years, but at twenty, I realized I didn't quite fit the mold of the typical American teenager. Kaufman's passions were my passions too. The difference was that I hadn't begun to pursue those passions yet.

My grandparents and parents supported my newfound identity as a birder, lending me and giving me the necessary optical accessories, including binoculars, a Swarovski telescope, and a Canon 300-mm digital camera for wildlife photography. I read books on the subject, including Mark Obmascik's *The Big Year*, which described the 1998 competition among three American birders to break the record for most species seen in North America in a single year.

Birding has been a growing American pastime ever since Frank Chapman founded the Christmas Bird Counts in 1900. More than a century later, some sources claim that 100 million Americans watch birds. However, a small percentage of these people are competitive birdwatchers, known as birders. The sport of birding is a unique recreation that has not only caught on in North America, but also throughout the world. Unlike other sports, there are no organized professional associations to promote competitive events among birders, so there are no true professional birding "athletes." A few professional birders, like Kenn Kaufman, earn a living by sharing their expertise as guides, tour leaders, and authors. Organized birding competitions do exist as team events that raise money for environmental conservation. Some examples include the New Jersey Audubon Society's World Series of Birding and the Texas Birding Classic.

Competitive individuals in the birding world join the American Birding Association (ABA) and publish their birding accomplishments in the form of list totals in one of the Association's annual publications reserved for this purpose. The list categories ("competitions") include Life Lists (a tally of species observed and identified in a birder's lifetime) for a variety of geographic regions at smaller and smaller scales beginning with the World, then continents, countries, and states. The ABA also publishes day list totals known as Big Days, a team event carried out in a

24-hour period beginning at midnight (the national highest Big Day total is 260 species, accomplished in 2008 by Cameron Cox, Ken Behrens, Pete Hosner, and Michael Retter in Texas). The ABA promotes a strict set of listing rules and birding ethics to ensure that the welfare of the birds takes priority over the obsessive needs of ABA members.

Within states, competitive birders join state-wide birding organizations. In Colorado, the Colorado Field Ornithologists (C.F.O.) periodically publishes birders' Life List totals not only for the state of Colorado, but also for several regions within the state (e.g. East of the Continental Divide), and for all sixty-four counties. A popular state-level competition is the Annual List. Most competitive Colorado birders strive each year to find 300 species in the state. When I started writing this book, the Annual List record for Colorado was an astounding 391 species, established in 2008 by Andrew Spencer, a twenty-three-year-old birding phenom now leading tours in the jungles and cloud forests of Ecuador.

In competitive birding, there are no specialized judges or officials. Lists are compiled by the listers themselves using the honor system. The community of competitive birders serves as referees, and the integrity of a birder's list is rooted in the quality of a birder's identification skills. As with all issues based on integrity, a birder's reputation is precious. Once lost, it is practically impossible to rebuild, and any published list total by the unfortunate birder will be doubted and ridiculed by many of his/her peers. The birding community can be ruthless, making competitive birding a difficult nut to crack for beginners.

Not all competitive birding pits one birder against another. Many birders compete with themselves, trying to increase their various list totals for their own personal goals. This type of competition is free of the judgmental scrutiny of the birding community.

Competitive birding has blossomed with the advent of the Internet and modern communication systems. With new information now transmitted instantaneously, birders can react to a rare bird sighting within minutes. Friends share news of their finds via text messaging and cellular phone calls. The entire community is generally aware within hours through telephone-recorded rare-bird alerts and widely distributed email messages sent out on birding listserves.

Advances in communication tools like cell phones, wireless Internet, and ipods provided the tools that enabled me to break into the birding world relatively late in my life at age nineteen (many of the top competitive birders began developing their skills as small children), and to join the ranks of competitive birders. By age twenty-six, I would attempt the biggest birding feat in Colorado. I would embark upon a Colorado Big Year, a year-long effort to break the Annual List record for Colorado.

CHAPTER TWO

How I Became a Birder

I SAW THE ANNOUNCEMENT IN the Loveland Reporter Herald on a crisp, cold November morning in Northern Colorado: Special Field Trip to see a rare Kelp Gull. I had never heard of a Kelp Gull. I had no clue that a Kelp Gull was particularly special in Colorado, or anywhere else in the United States for that matter.

I felt like I knew birds pretty well from growing up in the foothills of the Rockies. I could call in Wild Turkeys, a skill I learned while hunting in the hills with my father and grandfather. My name is Cole Wild, from Loveland, Colorado. The Wild family homesteaded at Storm Mountain west of Loveland when Colorado was the American frontier. We have been hunting turkey, mule deer, and elk in the remote foothills in Larimer County for generations. My mother is a school librarian. My father is a ditch rider for an irrigation company (water is a big deal in Colorado).

The men in my family are mountain men. We know magpies and hawks and eagles like we know our own pet cats and dogs and our chickens, goats, and horses. But that Saturday morning in the local newspaper, my sense of awareness of our natural surroundings was challenged. Kelp Gull? I had seen "seagulls" in town at Lake Loveland, a man-made water storage reservoir stocked for recreational fishing. I also knew from our hunting expeditions that gulls—later I would learn they were California Gulls—nested by the hundreds with American White Pelicans and Double-crested Cormorants at Walden Reservoir in Jackson County at 9000 feet elevation near the Wyoming border. These gulls and the other water birds—ducks, geese, shorebirds—were part of our Colorado landscape.

Not until I read the invitation to view this Kelp Gull among the gulls at Lake Loveland did it even occur to me that gulls were associated with oceans and seaweed (kelp is a type of seaweed that grows in great floating mats in the ocean). I had never traveled outside Colorado, except to visit my mother's family in Nebraska. I certainly never had gone anywhere close to an ocean or a sea coast.

The idea of attending this special field trip in November, 2003, intrigued me. I was nineteen years old, finished with high school, just starting to confront the world as a young man. I had a part-time job monitoring water quality in the Big Thompson River which flows from Rocky Mountain National Park downhill through Loveland and eastward through the Great Plains. I felt at home in the outdoors. The birds of the river were my friends—American Dippers, Common Mergansers, Mallards.

I had recently begun taking more notice of birds just a few months earlier after taking Tom Hewson's Environmental Science class in the spring semester of my senior year at Thompson Valley High School. Like most high school students, I thought our class objective of learning to identify 100 species of birds was a ridiculous waste of time. Then on a fishing trip to Big Creek Reservoir near Walden, I actually recognized one of those 100 species, a Black-crowned Night-Heron. And when I noticed another one, a brightly colored Western Tanager (bright yellow and black, with a scarlet head, Fig. 1) in the pines above our campsite, the birdwatching gene in me suddenly switched to the "on" position. From that day onward, I would begin to notice the birds around me, and even write down their names as I identified them.

By November, 2003, I had recorded observations of some 125 species. Kelp Gull, however, had not crossed my path of consciousness. Maybe I would meet some interesting people on this field trip. Perhaps there could be a nice girl interested in something like a Kelp Gull. At age nineteen, I was alert to any opportunity to meet women my age. 'What the heck,' I thought out-loud, 'let's see what this Kelp Gull is all about.'

I met the organizers of this group outing at the swim beach parking lot at Lake Loveland, about four miles from my house on the southwest outskirts of the city of Loveland. Nick Komar, representing the Fort Collins Audubon

7

Society, was a biologist from Fort Collins, the neighboring city north of Loveland. Chris Wood, representing the Colorado Field Ornithologists, was a young naturalist from Denver. The thirty or so trip attendees assembled from as far away as Wyoming and New Mexico. They carried binoculars around their necks, and most of them were well equipped with high-powered telescopes on sturdy tripods. Some wielded fancy cameras with long, telephoto lenses. Most of them were older than me, adults of a variety of ages and backgrounds. This one morning, they all seemed exceptionally single-minded. They were intently focused on finding this one single bird called Kelp Gull.

At first I felt out of place. I soon gleaned from the conversation that this one bird was from the coast of South America, from south of the equator! This wanderer was the first of its species to visit the interior U.S., and just a few others had visited coastal localities, mostly along the Gulf of Mexico. The novelty and uniqueness of the situation made sense to me.

As the search ensued (the Kelp Gull was not at Lake Loveland that morning, although it had been roosting there each night with hundreds of other local California Gulls and Ring-billed Gulls), I began to feel a surge of excitement. It was contagious from these birdwatchers. They explained to me their obsessive, competitive hobby of "birding"—trying to see as many species as they could, building personal lists of birds seen in countries, states, and even counties (there are sixty-four counties in Colorado alone). They explained that the trip leaders this morning were among some of the most skilled "birders" in the state of Colorado.

Within a couple of hours of searching local gull hangouts at lakes near Loveland, Brian Gibbons—a scout sent to check out the gulls at the county landfill—called in with exciting news. The Kelp Gull had been spotted! The convoy of vehicles rushed to the landfill. When we arrived, the gull flock had flown off, dispersing in a variety of directions. The group split up to check different possible destinations of the gulls. I stayed with Komar's group.

Just a few minutes later, Brian called again to inform us that Chris Wood had spotted the Kelp Gull at Horsetooth Reservoir, a ten-mile long, deep-water lake in the foothills just west of the landfill. A gull flock was floating on the water, resting from their foraging efforts at the county dump. Through telescopes, we viewed dozens of California, Ring-billed, and several Herring Gulls. The leaders pointed out two darker gulls, a smaller one with a blackish back called a Lesser Black-backed Gull, and next to it in the same scope view, a larger gull with an ink-black back and bright white head and underparts, sporting a massive yellow bill. This was the famous Kelp Gull. I recognized it from its picture in the paper. The birders were ecstatic. Hugs and congratulations spread through the group of satisfied birders. I didn't know it then, but I had just been hooked on birding.

Following the field trip, Nick and Chris and Brian invited me to look for other interesting birds. During the course of the afternoon, they showed me more rare gulls—Thayer's Gull and Mew Gull—and numerous other species that I had never heard of like Common and Pacific Loons. At the end of the afternoon, Chris Wood told me that if I bought the Sibley Guide to Birds, learned gulls, and went birding as often as I could then I could become as skilled a birder as he. Having the privilege of the distinguished company of these outstanding leaders of the Colorado birding world on my first organized birdwatching outing sealed the deal for me. Observing, listing, and photographing birds would become my principal passions of my young adulthood.

Over the next half-decade, Nick Komar became one of my mentors, taking me on numerous birding trips around Fort Collins and Loveland, as well as other destinations throughout the state of Colorado, and even Mexico and Ecuador. Chris Wood went on to work and study at Cornell University, where he spearheaded the gargantuan data collection project known as eBird. I would develop close friendships with other birding mentors: Andrew Spencer, Mark Peterson, Brandon Percival, and Tony Leukering. With each new outing in the company of these incredibly knowledgeable observers of Colorado's birds, I became a better birder.

The skills I learned from these teachers would qualify me for various ornithological employment opportunities over the years, bringing me to study birds in the grasslands of Colorado, Texas, and Mexico; to count migrating raptors in Florida; and to assess the effects of wind energy farms on birds in Texas and Pennsylvania. By the end of 2009, I was ready to attempt a feat never before accomplished in Colorado—observing 400 species in a single year!

Figure 1. A **Western Tanager** hooked me on birding

CHAPTER THREE

January

JANUARY 1ST IS AN ANNUAL Day of reflection for me: Where I have been; where I am going; what goals I shall set for myself this year; New Year's resolutions. On that fateful first day of 2010, I had no idea I would be embarking on a year-long journey to achieve what no one had ever achieved before, to challenge the limits of the human condition. I did not envision on that ordinary New Year's Day that I would soon be full steam ahead, all systems go, pedal to the metal in hot pursuit of the Colorado Big Year record of 391 bird species observed (seen or heard) by a mere mortal within a single year.

I began the year all of twenty-five years old, single, living at my parents' house, spinning my wheels professionally. I had tried studying for a college degree, but attempts at Colorado State University and Front Range Community College were fruitless. Higher education and I are like oil and water—we just don't get along. For about a year, I had been working in a dead-end job as a lab technician in a plasma donation center in Fort Collins.

New Year's Resolution Number One—get a better job!

'If I get a better job,' I thought, 'I could afford to find my own place to live.' Resolution Number Two—move out of my parents' house. With a good job and a nice apartment, maybe I could finally land a serious relationship. Resolution Number Three—find a girlfriend. Ideally I could find a girlfriend who was compatible with my interests and hobbies. It seems like few women my age are passionate about birding. I had yet to meet a girlfriend who would tolerate my weekend trips to find more bird species in Colorado's remote counties. Resolution Number Four—concentrate my birding in 2010 to maximize my county Life Lists. Resolution Number Five—become the top e-birder in Colorado.

E-bird (or eBird) is an electronic database housed at Cornell University's Lab of Ornithology. Bird watchers all over the world are encouraged to submit their sightings checklists through a friendly webpage (www.ebird. org). These checklists are analyzed by some behind-the-scenes computer formulas to generate incredibly useful bird abundance charts for just about any location you can imagine. The idea has recently caught on among birders. The data being generated is accomplishing in minutes what used to require years of research.

The eBird central computer manages each contributor's sightings, so if you submit all your sightings, the computer can tell you all your Life List totals for any location or time period. In 2009 I spent countless hours importing my lists

of birds seen since I began keeping track with handwrit-
ten lists for every new location and date, which added up
to thousands of checklists. The eBird team, comprised of
a small number of computer whizzes who are also birders, recognizes the biggest contributor of new lists each
month, and I was hoping my gargantuan efforts to input
data into the computer would someday be recognized on
the face page of the website.

While I never earned "E-birder of the Month" accolades, my efforts were noticed by the eBird staff in New
York and I would later be asked by Chris Wood to be a
volunteer report checker for Colorado.

Well, thinking back to those resolutions a year later, I
must admit that I was not able to achieve any of those lofty
goals, in spite of significant efforts! Does anyone ever ful-
fill their New Year's resolutions? I certainly never have.

I began my birding year with the goal of finding 100
species by the end of January. This number of species represents about twenty per-cent of the avian biodiversity of
Colorado. But it is more than half of the bird species present in the state in the dead of winter. Most of Colorado's
birds either pass through the state during spring and fall
migrations, or visit during the summer breeding season,
when food for birds is much more plentiful.

During January, I would find most of the usual winter
residents and visitors and several rare species, including a
Snowy Owl (Fig. 2) that made a cameo appearance to the

delight of hundreds of spectators near Colorado Springs. These beautiful white ghosts normally hunt lemmings in the arctic tundra, but when rodent populations crash in the North, they wander far and wide in search of rodent prey, many crossing the Canadian border into the lower forty-eight. A few reach Colorado every winter, but finding them in the expanses of Colorado's eastern plains is like finding a needle in a haystack, and when the plains are snow-covered, spotting one is even tougher.

I convinced my non-birder brother (Cody) to join me on January 11th for the four-hour round-trip road trip to find the owl, which had been "staked out" at its favorite diurnal roost on the roof of a rural farmhouse. Several hours later, after seeing the owl, we visited a stretch of the Cache La Poudre River in Weld County where a rare Red-shouldered Hawk, a vagrant from the Midwest, had also been staked out.

By the end of the month, I had scored 122 species for my Colorado Year List, including several other staked out rarities. These were White-winged Crossbill (Fig. 3; a pair that would later raise young) at Grandview Cemetery in Fort Collins, Great Black-backed Gull at Pueblo Reservoir (an East Coast bird, but one resides in Pueblo every winter), and three West Coast visitors: Golden-crowned Sparrow at the Red Rocks Trading Post bird feeders near Denver, Pacific Wren at Fountain Creek Nature Center in El Paso County, and Glaucous-winged Gull at the Erie Landfill in Weld County.

CHAPTER FOUR

February

FEBRUARY IS A MONTH OF transition in Colorado. Spring migration is just getting started, even though winter is in full swing. In fact, February is the beginning of the snowiest three months of the year in Colorado. But spring melodies from birds feeling the love in the air begin to filter into the consciousness of hibernating bears, and birders. Most Colorado birders will remain dormant until May, when multitudes emerge to enjoy the colorful songbirds such as warblers, tanagers, orioles, and buntings, at the height of spring migration.

In February, many year-round songbirds take up residence on their breeding territories. For example, brazen male Red-winged Blackbirds are already defending their patch of cattails, and American Robins and House Finches begin to serenade their mates in the landscaped glades of residential neighborhoods up and down the Colorado Front Range. At Grandview Cemetery in Fort Collins, numerous Pine Siskins initiated their early breeding cycle, along with the pair of White-winged Crossbills, which were highly celebrated by birders from all over Colorado.

Their daily activities would be monitored intently and described by their discoverer, David Leatherman, for the virtual Colorado birding community in the electronic pages of COBirds, the Colorado birding email listserve established by the Colorado Field Ornithologists.

COBirds would play an important role in facilitating my Colorado Big Year, but I am getting ahead of myself. The pursuit of Andrew Spencer's record of 391 bird species in Colorado had not yet taken root in my mind, although the seed had been planted by my successful list total in January of 122 species. That seed would be watered and fertilized by a number of rare birds found during this month. For example, after enjoying the spectacle of the nesting crossbills on February 16th, a lone Bohemian Waxwing paused briefly among the budding crowns of the numerous giant cottonwood trees. During some winters, these frugivorous boreal waxwings descend upon Colorado in the thousands, but this was the only sighting for this winter.

That day, February 16th, was a special day of birding. Every once in a blue moon, the birding gods smile down upon the Earth and bestow special gifts to the most devout birders, those of us who spend enough time outdoors peering through our binoculars to be in the right place and time to witness these gifts. On this day, after the brief but highly successful visit to the cemetery, I ventured east from Fort Collins to the prairie expanses of the Pawnee

National Grasslands, where I would find a Sage Thrasher (presumably an early spring migrant), a rare Long-eared Owl (Fig. 4), as well as the expected Lapland Longspurs. These drab granivorous birds that visit from the Arctic tundra November to March are always a challenge to find among the hordes of Horned Larks that inhabit the prairie grasslands. Even more of a challenge is the rare Snow Bunting, but I wouldn't find one of these visitors from the far North until later in the month farther east in Logan County. Later in this day, I re-located two rare winter gulls, Glaucous Gull and Iceland Gull, that had been reported among the hundreds of common Ring-billed and Herring Gulls near the Erie landfill north of Denver. Iceland Gull was only added to the state list in the year 2000.

A successful birding day like February 16th can change a person's life, just like the day seven years ago when I noticed the beauty of the Western Tanager and became hooked on birds. On February 16th, I sensed that the birding deities had selected me to be witness to the avian wonders of the natural world, at least in the state of Colorado. The seed of the Colorado Big Year was growing, sending shoots toward the surface of my consciousness.

CHAPTER FIVE

March

I STARTED THIS MONTH WITH 140 species, well below the number of species that can be found in Colorado during the winter (about 200 species). To find all the species of Colorado, it is necessary to visit all the diverse habitats that the state offers: The eastern grasslands; the Chihuahuan Desert of the southeast portion of the state; the pygmy forests of Piñon Pine and juniper trees that carpet extensive areas of rolling hills in the southern half of the state; the extensive Ponderosa Pine forests of the southwest; the riparian canyons of the Sonoran Desert plateau near the Utah border; the sub-alpine spruce-fir forests and sagebrush grasslands of the high Rockies; the alpine tundra at the highest altitudes (above 11,000 feet); the riparian corridors of the various rivers and associated wetlands; and the extensive patchwork of inland lakes and reservoirs.

In March, I began to focus on adding some of the more habitat-specialized species to my annual list. This would require more travel. I devoted most of my birding time this month to tracking down mountain birds including grouse species, rosy finches, and small owls. These birds are responsible for most of Colorado's booming birdwatching tourism business. Each spring, numerous organized tours attract hundreds of birding tourists to find these species, which can be found more easily all together in Colorado than in any other state. Most of these tours visit the state in April to take advantage of the warmer temperatures in the mountains. Tour companies that bring birders to Colorado include Elderhostel, Wings, Field Guides, ObservTours, High Lonesome Tours, and Quetzal Tours. I hope to lead some of these tours one day.

To be an effective birding tour leader one must know the territory (and its bird life) intimately, knowledge gained by many trips to the tour locations at a variety of seasons. During the last few years, I had the opportunity to visit many locations in Colorado with local birders who had served as professional tour guides, and these mentors imparted their knowledge to me, at no charge (which was good, because I would not have had the money to take a tour, or even hire a birding guide).

This month, I would be the tour guide, for my own family members. My first tour departed my house in Loveland with my father, Bruce Wild, at 11 p.m. on March 12th. We headed west through the mountains on State Highway 14, a slow, curvy road that follows the Cache La Poudre River canyon for sixty miles, finally crossing the first mountain pass at 10,000 feet. Cameron Pass is the border between

Larimer and Jackson Counties, and is perhaps the best location in Colorado to hear the eerie midnight tremolo—a rapid series of low hoots—of the Boreal Owl. The night was frigid and calm, and the starlight was intense.

We stopped several times on both sides of the pass, and detected several Boreal Owls incessantly hooting their territorial call, which is given frequently at night throughout the spring courting season from February to May. The call is often confused by midsummer campers with the sound of displaying Wilson's Snipes in flight overhead, given at dawn and dusk. In a bizarre twist, the call is most similar to that of the Moustached Antpitta of the South American jungles. It is heard frequently on the soundtracks of numerous television shows and movies that need eerie bird calls in the background.

At the bottom of the pass we entered the great mountain-ringed grassland plateau known as North Park. Crossing more than fifty miles of high mountain grasslands, Highway 14 ends at the Continental Divide, and the Grand County line. From here, we continued west on U.S. Highway 40, crossing Rabbit Ears Pass into Routt County. The normally bustling mountain resort town of Steamboat Springs was quiet at 4 a.m. We followed the Yampa River valley westward another thirty miles to the hamlet of Hayden, where we turned north on Routt County Road 80C, a dirt ribbon of a road that goes to nowhere fast. Leaving the river valley, the road rolls over a series of treeless hills covered with a quilt of alternating cattle pastures, sagebrush grasslands, and Gambel Oak shrublands. This is the remote homeland of the montane sub-species of Sharp-tailed Grouse.

Rumor has it that the prairie subspecies occasionally incurs into the low-elevation grasslands of northern Larimer and Weld Counties in north-central Colorado. However, this subspecies is reliably found farther north and east in the long-grass prairies of eastern Montana, eastern Wyoming, western Nebraska, South and North Dakota, northern sections of Minnesota, Wisconsin, Michigan, most of Canada, and extending westward to Alaska.

At 5 a.m. we could go no farther as the snow-covered roads would not allow even my Dad's 4×4 pickup truck to advance. The sky was beginning to brighten, and through the frigid sub-zero mountain air we could hear bubbling and squawking of distant chicken-like birds. The Sharp-tailed Grouse were assembled at their courtship grounds, a gathering known as a "lek."

Several mountain grouse species find their mates at leks, communal strutting grounds where alpha males puff out their chests, display their feathers in a variety of entertaining postures, and generally show off to the local females. The females select the best males to pass their genes on to the next generation of grouse, ensuring the survival of the species.

Survival in the harsh conditions of the high Rocky Mountain grasslands is no simple matter. Aside from the inhumane climate, these large meaty birds must contend with hungry mountain lions and coyotes, rapacious Golden Eagles, and unrelenting blood-thirsty mosquitoes. These hazards seem daunting, but the true enemies of these birds are human beings. Aside from pressure from upland game hunters, ranchers seem to be ever expanding their cattle pastures, causing the native shrub habitat of the grouse to shrink.

In some areas farther north in Wyoming and Montana, oil and natural gas drilling is causing more headaches for the Greater Sage-Grouse. Shallow ponds created by the drilling operations breed *Culex tarsalis* mosquitoes that carry West Nile virus. This virus that can cause encephalitis in a small percentage of people and horses also causes fatal infections in 100% of the Greater Sage-Grouse that become infected. Crazy.

As the sun warmed up the rolling hills north of Hayden (known locally as California Park), we spotted the distant Sharp-tailed Grouse through my telescope. Mission accomplished. Turning back, we stopped mid-morning in a patch of sagebrush at Coalmont in North Park, where a Greater Sage-Grouse lek is well known to birders. The displaying sage-grouse disperse shortly after sunrise. Fortunately, some of the giant grouse were milling about, feeding among the sage.

More mountain specialty birds, only found at high elevation, mingled around a house in Gould, close to Cameron Pass. A cluster of bird feeders among Lodgepole Pines provided a smorgasbord for Gray Jays, Pine Grosbeaks (Fig. 5), and a small flock of Brown-capped Rosy-Finches. A few Black Rosy-Finches, a species that only visits Colorado during the winter months, had joined the flock.

The tour, normally conducted over three days or so for tourists, lasted less than twenty-four hours.

My next tour was with my brother Cody on March 21st. After a couple of fun birding trips in January to southern Colorado to see the Snowy Owl and other cool birds like Greater Roadrunner, Cody was up for searching for another cool bird, also snow-white like the owl. We would search for White-tailed Ptarmigan, disguised as snow in their winter plumage high in the Rocky Mountain snow-covered tundra at Guanella Pass. We drove four hours from our home in Loveland to reach the pass, high above the quaint, former silver-mining town of Georgetown.

At the pass, we encountered a blinding blizzard. We began to hike around the pass using snowshoes to avoid falling through four-foot snow drifts. We searched in vain for the ptarmigan among the willow shrubs which provide both food and shelter for the snow-colored chicken-like birds. The blasting wind of the blizzard forced a quick retreat. Cody didn't join me on any more birding tours the rest of the year.

I tried one more March mountain tour the following weekend with my friend Sol Miller. I found the ptarmigan readily among the willows at Loveland Pass close to the Eisenhower Tunnel west of Denver. Later in the day in the hills west of Fort Collins, we found and photographed a Northern Pygmy-Owl (Fig. 6) in Rist Canyon. Then at Cameron Pass we heard a total of seven Boreal Owls on the Jackson County side. We managed to glimpse one fly across the road near the pass. Most exciting that night was the haunting howl of a wolf from one side of the highway, followed by a chorus of yelps from some frightened coyotes on the other side of the road. Returning home to Loveland via the Poudre Canyon, we were rewarded with a tooting Northern Saw-whet Owl along the way.

March was a month of extreme mountain birding (when I wasn't working at the plasma center in Fort Collins). I only chased one staked-out rarity, a migrating Sage Sparrow (Fig. 7) that had stopped over for a brief, but extended stay at Chatfield State Park near Denver on March 20th. I added 34 species to my Colorado annual list, ending the month at 174 species.

The shoots of the Big Year that were growing towards the surface of my consciousness were just about to break out of the unused part of my brain.

CHAPTER SIX

April

I STARTED THE MONTH OF April enthused about my birding exploits of 2010, but I still hadn't fully embraced the concept of attempting a Big Year. Andrew Spencer's record of 391 species still seemed way beyond reach. I had begun previous years at a similar pace as 2010, and ended with Year List totals of 369 in 2009 and 370 in 2008. So I continued working on my New Year's resolution of improving my county Life List totals.

I had not forgotten about my other New Year's resolutions either. My job in particular was beginning to get old. I had dated one of my co-workers for a while, but that relationship did not work out too well, and now I tried to avoid her at work, a situation that made going to work some days quite uncomfortable. 'If I left that job,' I thought, 'then I'd have more time for birding, at least until I find a new job.'

My first birding opportunity came Friday, April 2nd (I traded for a Saturday shift with a coworker). I joined Jessica Brauch on a "chicken run." Jess would be leading prairie-chicken and grouse tours later in the month for

Quetzal Tours, and had not yet been to the leks of the Lesser and Greater Prairie-Chickens. These birds, like the closely related grouse, are targets of eco-tourists. In a long day-trip from Fort Collins, we made the 450-mile loop through Prowers County near the Oklahoma border and Yuma County near the Nebraska border to find these skulking prairie grouse species.

Besides chasing grouse, Colorado birders in April are keen on finding gulls. Yes, seagulls. California Gulls actually are not really sea gulls. They nest not on sea-shores or sea cliffs, but rather on low sandy islands of inland lakes and reservoirs. Thousands of these large gray and white gulls accumulate in populated sections of Colorado (mainly near cities along the Front Range) from February to April, once the lakes thaw. They spend their days stuffing themselves with delicious morsels of garbage at the various landfills located near the cities of Pueblo, Colorado Springs, Denver, Boulder, Longmont, Loveland, and Fort Collins. They supplement their diet of garbage with fresh fish and crawdads that abound in the numerous lakes and reservoirs of the Front Range, often aided by the fishing prowess of thousands of Common Mergansers and Common Goldeneyes. These diving ducks follow massive schools of minnow and once they bring a piscine victim to the surface, they are pounced upon by a thieving gull, only to repeat the process over and over again!

In spring, the California Gulls are decked out in

spanking-fresh breeding plumage of crisp white feathers on their heads and necks, with handsomely painted faces featuring bright lipstick-red eye-rings, gape (the mouth lining, like fine lips), and gonydeal spot, the bright mark near the tip of the bill that will be used by their chicks later in the summer to induce parental regurgitation for meals. The red spot stands out on an otherwise bright yellow bill, which matches nicely the bright yellow legs and feet of the California Gulls in breeding condition. The legs and feet become a bluish-gray at other times of the year.

Naturally, these handsome gulls can't help flirting with each other in the warming spring weather, preparing for the upcoming breeding season. The larger males frequently hop on top of the backs of the smaller females in a sort of rehearsal for copulation, which will come later. The gulls also spend much time loafing on the lakes and sandbars, and sleeping. Ah, what a life.

When it is finally time to leave the scrumptious food scraps of the Front Range cities (at the end of April), these gulls will disperse to breeding colonies at Riverside Reservoir in Weld County, Walden Reservoir in Jackson County, sometimes Antero Reservoir in Park County, and other colonies farther north in Wyoming.

The California Gulls are accompanied by thousands of Ring-billed Gulls which behave much the same way, but disperse entirely to Wyoming and other points north of Colorado for breeding. Likewise, the much smaller, black-headed Franklin's Gulls disperse to nesting grounds in the prairie potholes of North Dakota and Canada.

Several fascinating gull species make their way to Colorado from Arctic nesting areas. These would include the large Herring Gull, the tiny Bonaparte's Gull, and a group of pale, "white-winged gulls" whose paleness is suggestive of the ice and snow of the polar ice cap. The white-winged gulls always stand out as odd-balls in Colorado in April. But April is a time when gulls are on the move, and for some reason, these rare gulls always seem to appear, albeit in very small numbers. The white-winged gulls lack the typical black wingtips of most of the gull species I have mentioned so far. White-winged gulls include the largest and whitest Glaucous Gull, and its smaller twin, Iceland Gull, as well as Thayer's Gull, which resembles an Iceland Gull with darker wingtips or a Herring Gull with paler wingtips, and finally Glaucous-winged Gull, which resembles Glaucous Gull but with gray wingtips.

For some reason, these Arctic gulls seem to be visiting Colorado's reservoirs and landfills with increasing frequency. I cannot say whether this is because Colorado has become more attractive to gulls, or because the northern Arctic Ocean shores of Canada, the usual winter haunts of many of these white-winged gulls, no longer satisfy all of these birds. Regardless, their visits are candy for the competitive birder, and they often provide a welcome identification challenge, especially in spring.

Unlike the sharply plumaged California Gulls and Ring-billed Gulls in spring, the odd-ball white-winged gulls are often quite messy in their plumage. They seem to mostly be young birds in sub-adult, mottled plumages. Furthermore, because the birds of the high latitudes breed later than Colorado breeders, these gulls have not yet begun their spring "pre-alternate" molt. Thus, by April, their feathers often appear worn and sometimes bleached and faded, giving them an even whiter appearance. Because of the odd plumages caused by molt and feather wear and fading, some individual gulls can have confusing or cryptic plumage features, and may not be definitively identified.

Lucky for me, 2010 turned out to be a great year for these white-winged gulls. In April, Thayer's Gull was present in small numbers, with about a dozen being a typical number observed if one spent the whole day visiting gull hangouts. On Sunday April 4th, I spent a morning looking at gulls in Weld County with Nick Komar in an unsuccessful search for a mega-rare Black-headed Gull (vagrant from Eurasia or perhaps Canada's east coast) that had been reported by Fort Collins birder Josh Bruenning the previous day. He had seen it sitting in a recently tilled field with other black-headed Franklin's Gulls and the abundant white-headed Ring-billed Gulls, near the North Weld County Landfill north of Windsor. The area was a gold mine for gulls this spring. That morning, Nick and I spotted two Iceland Gulls and a Glaucous-winged Gull at nearby Black Hollow Reservoir, and then at the land-fill proper, a second sighting of two Iceland Gulls with a Glaucous Gull.

We would return a couple of mornings later with a birding buddy from Denver, Joe Roller, in a second unsuc-cessful search for the Black-headed Gull. This time at the landfill, we found Glaucous Gull, and a second large sub-adult white-winged gull, sporting a dingy gray back. Its bulky shape and all dark bill suggested another Glaucous-winged Gull which perhaps had begun to acquire its gray back during its pre-alternate molt. Alternatively, the dingy gray back and otherwise white plumage may have been a faded, worn sub-adult (in its second spring) Slaty-backed Gull, from the Bering Sea of Alaska and Siberia. Unfortunately, this is one of those messy gulls that we could not identify based on the looks (and photographs) that we were able to obtain. If it were a Slaty-backed Gull, it would be only the second record ever for Colorado. The first and only accepted record of this species for the state was an adult discovered by Fort Collins birder David Leatherman in Loveland (less than twenty miles away) where it stayed for about three weeks in late March and early April of 2000.

Gulls seem to wander great distances off-course more than almost any other type of bird. Apparently they are very strong fliers. Take for example the Kelp Gull of 2003, which apparently wandered to Colorado from as far away as Peru in South America. Why would a bird wander so far from home? Perhaps these wanderers are searching for better feeding sites. Perhaps they are simply blown off course during strong winds or a storm, and then become lost. Perhaps due to a genetic malfunction these wanderers have an abnormal sense of direction for their migratory flights. Perhaps, like the literary character Jonathan Livingston Seagull, they fly long-distances off-course because they can, and they have an irresistible curiosity, a drive to explore new areas.

The propensity for gulls and other birds to occasionally turn up thousands of miles from home is perhaps one of the most attractive aspects of birding for the competitive bird watcher. These vagrants provide the opportunity to continually add to one's lists; the possibility of additional conquest is always present. These birds also make birding more interesting, providing a new challenge with every bird sighting. Careful observers must consider all possibilities, including remote ones, when identifying even the most mundane of familiar birds. For example, a California Gull in its 3rd winter appears like an adult in many respects, but it can have a very thick black tail band, recalling a Black-tailed Gull.

Black-tailed Gull is a common gull in northeastern Asia that sporadically turns up in coastal locations (and even more rarely in the interior) of North America. It has never been identified in Colorado, but like other gulls, some will wander away from their normal haunts. One of these wanderers may follow other gulls to the shores of a Colorado lake. Birders in Colorado could easily overlook an adult Black-tailed Gull, passing it off as a third-year California Gull. Immature birds in sub-adult plumage are even more cryptic.

Most birders, even competitive ones, will admit that they tend to ignore gulls, considering them less interesting than colorful warblers and tanagers. Fortunately for me, all my mentors have been larophiles—birders who take a particular interest in birds of the family Laridae, the gull family. While all competitive birders jump at the opportunity to add a new gull species to their various lists, only larophiles study these creatures sufficiently to recognize an oddity among them. The Slaty-backed Gull of 2000 and the Kelp Gull of 2003 are examples of such oddities. The larophiles are always on the lookout for the next exotic gull species from distant shores that will add yet another species to Colorado's state bird list.

CHAPTER SEVEN
A Big Year

AS THE EARTH CONTINUED TO spin in its orbit around the sun, more and more migratory birds were returning to Colorado to establish breeding territories or stop over for refueling in transit to points further north.

Colorado lies between the major migration routes along the Pacific coast (the Pacific Flyway) and the Mississippi River valley (the Mississippi Flyway) so the sheer number of migrants passing through is not impressive. Birds that migrate over Colorado are considered to be on the western fringe of the Central Flyway, although the whole 'flyway' concept is really a big generalization fraught with misconceptions, like any other generalization. For example, migrating birds are found everywhere, not just along their recognized migration flyways.

Many of the more uncommon migrants that grace Colorado during spring and fall migrations, such as Rose-breasted Grosbeak or Broad-winged Hawk, represent a minority of their respective populations, the proverbial tails of the bell curve that represents their species' normal geographic distribution and abundance. However the rarest Colorado migrants, such as Swainson's Warbler or Curlew Sandpiper, are individuals with unorthodox migratory bearings. These are frequently termed "off-course" or "overshoots" or "confused" or "disoriented." These birds have become separated from the other individuals in their population. To the competitive birder eager to expand his/her listing conquests, they are more than welcome. Because these out-of-place migrants are encountered so infrequently, one cannot expect to find many of them, if any at all. However, as a birding community with thousands of eyes ever aware of flitting wings in the periphery, we do find these rare gems.

Each morning during the spring migration period (migration is really all the time, for some species are migrating through Colorado on any day of the year), I would check my email, especially messages downloaded from the COBirds listserve, for an announcement of a rarity. The Black-headed Gull from April 3rd was such an announcement, although I was not lucky enough to re-find it. (In fact, no one ever reported re-finding this bird.)

Another announcement came very early in the morning on April 9th. A Yellow-throated Warbler (Fig. 8), hundreds of miles off-course to the west of its usual breeding grounds and migration routes, was spotted at Crow Valley Campground, a migrant trap (i.e. a popular stopover for migrating birds) in the Pawnee National Grassland in eastern Weld County. I had just enough time to chase the warbler, and get back to Fort Collins in time for work! This campground was a magnet for migrating birds. From a birds-eye view, it was an island of trees in a grassland sea, offering the promise of both food and shelter. Today it was quiet except for this one off-course overshoot. It was still too early for the major northward movement of songbirds. However, the push of migrating land birds was just a few weeks away, and this spring would bring many more overshoots and vagrants, more so than most years.

On Saturday, April 10th, I ventured to southwestern Colorado to work on my Saguache County Life List. I was joined by Colorado Springs birder Mark Peterson. Mark was a fiercely competitive county lister and in 2009 I had joined him on many long birding days carefully planned to maximize both his Year List and county lists from all over the state. Mark had held the annual Year List record for Colorado with 390 species before Andrew Spencer broke that record by one species in 2008. I had learned a lot birding with Andrew in 2008, but after Andrew left Colorado to become a tour leader in South America, I began birding more frequently with Mark and his buddies Brad Steger and Brandon Percival.

In Saguache County, Mark and I visited a known lek site for the threatened Gunnison Sage-Grouse. We also chased a rare bird for Rio Grande County in the San Luis Valley of south central Colorado: a Tundra Swan at Monte Vista National Wildlife Refuge.

On Saturday, April 24th, I combined county listing with year listing, visiting the southeast corner of
Colorado. For this trip, I joined forces with Dan Maynard
from Colorado Springs. Dan was a young birder (about
my age) who had recently returned to his home state of
Colorado to pursue a career in field ornithology. He told
me he was between jobs and for the present planned to
do a lot of birding all over Colorado. He had become an
avid birder in college and now had a goal of seeing every
bird he could in Colorado. We found many county Life
Birds and Colorado Year Birds that day. Some of the rarer
species were Carolina Wren and Harris's Sparrow at the
riparian grove behind Lamar Community College, Little
Blue Heron at Sheridan Lake in Kiowa County, Dunlin
at Lake Cheraw, and Caspian Tern at Rocky Ford State
Wildlife Area.

On the long five-hour drive back to Loveland that
night, I began thinking about my job, my birding goals,
the great birds I had been seeing.... and Dan Maynard.
From his posts to COBirds, I knew that Dan had been
seeing a lot of rare bird species in Colorado this year. I
suspected that he was willing to travel throughout the
state. I had run into him looking for rare gulls in northern Colorado in February. He probably had seen the adult
Yellow-crowned Night-Heron (Fig. 9) that I had chased
April 19th at Fountain Creek Regional Park near Colorado
Springs. I knew Dan was planning on spending the rest of

the weekend in southeast Colorado looking for more rare migrants. My competitive juices began to flow. Without a job, Dan would surely be able to make a run for the state Year List record, and with the great year for rare birds that 2010 was turning out to be, he could conceivably break the record, or if not, perhaps still score the best Year List for 2010. I had achieved this honor in 2009, and the thought of a newcomer to the local birding scene out-trumping me was intolerable.

Competitive birders are often considered obsessive, much the same as any avid collector. That night as I drove northward on the deserted State Highway 71, I realized what I must do. I would attempt to break the annual list record myself, a Colorado Big Year! The seed had finally sprouted, shooting forth into my consciousness. I immediately began fertilizing the seedling with ideas and plans.

I plotted my strategy for the remainder of the spring migration. I would adjust my work schedule to three long days, leaving Friday through Monday free. With the consecutive days available for birding, I would be able to take longer trips and spend more time in the more remote counties, where I could make real progress on my Big Year and on my county Life Lists. Over the next few days I configured my iPhone to be able to send and receive emails, so I could check COBirds reports at any time. I had recently signed on as a volunteer editor for eBird reports in northern Colorado, so I knew I would receive eBird alerts for rarities on my phone too. And I uploaded the Sibley Guide for Birds of North America, a pictorial field guide, and various digitized bird song collections. Now I was armed for my assault on the Big Year record.

I began executing my strategic plans on Friday, April 30th, returning to southeast Colorado. Needless to say, its location farthest south in the state, and closest to the Mississippi Flyway, makes this region notorious for hosting the earliest waves of land bird migrants reaching Colorado. To meet the migrants, dozens of Front Range birders would be visiting the array of well-known migrant traps and birding hotspots this weekend, many arriving early as I had. As prepared as I was, I would take full advantage of any rare find to serve my newfound cause. Little did I know that April 30th, 2010, would be a migration extravaganza, destined for the historical archives of the collective Colorado birding psyche—it was a truly amazing day for rare migrants, qualifying as a Colorado fallout. The birds were not numerous like they would be along the Texas or Louisiana coasts during a migration fallout, but the variety of species was unmatched for a spring day in Colorado.

That fateful day I would see White-eyed Vireo, Yellow-throated Vireo, two Nashville Warblers, three Northern Parula, two Black-throated Blue Warblers, two Townsend's Warblers, Prairie Warbler, two Hooded Warblers, and Summer Tanager, among others. Most of these were seen in the company of a group of about a dozen birders, informally led by Denver birder Joey Kellner, at locations that included Lamar Community College, Locust Grove at Neenoshe Reservoir, Tempel Grove, and Lamar's Fairmount Cemetery.

I would end the month with 259 Year Birds (and 218 species seen in the month of April alone).

CHAPTER EIGHT
May

MAY IS BY MANY ACCOUNTS the best month for birding in Colorado. Every local patch of habitat hosts numerous land birds that stop to rest from their migration odyssey, en route from lush tropical wintering grounds to temperate breeding territories. Bird watchers who seek these feathered treasures appear in the same local patches, many breaking out their binoculars and cameras for the first time since the last spring migration. Land birds in their multicolored breeding ("alternate") plumages can be breathtaking, and their spectacle at the peak of spring migration entices more outdoorsmen and outdoorswomen to practice the sport of bird watching than at any other time of year.

Many birders spend most of their time studying the bird happenings in just a few locations, generally near their homes. These locations are termed "local patches," and the local birders associated with each patch become the experts on anything and everything that relates to the birds of the local patch. One year (2005) I tried to visit Dixon Reservoir in Larimer County every day during spring and fall migration.

Dixon Reservoir is a small man-made reservoir about a half-mile in length, and a tenth of a mile wide at the western edge of the Great Plains, at the foot of the first wave of hills that flank the Rocky Mountains. It lies at an altitude of one mile above sea level, in a shallow, arid, tree-less valley littered with the raised mounds that form the entrance to burrows dug out by Black-tail Prairie-Dogs. The prairie-dog colony here sustains a population of several hundred animals, at least. These cute critters spend all day grazing the sparse prairie grasses that blanket the clay-dominated soil of the valley floor, along with stunted, miniature prickly pear, barrel cacti, and scattered agave plants. The prairie-dogs are really large ground squirrels. They feed actively during the day, never straying far from their burrow entrances, permitting a rapid retreat to the security of their subterranean burrows in the face of danger. Several prairie dogs at any one moment sit vertically on their short hind legs in sharp watch for their primary predators: Golden Eagles and Ferruginous Hawks. Other large raptors are commonly seen here as well, particularly Red-tailed Hawks and Prairie Falcons.

Eastern Cottontails and Meadow Voles share this eco-system with the prairie-dogs, and are the choice prey of the resident Red-tailed Hawks. American Kestrels hunt the voles and a variety of mouse species, as well as large insects like grasshoppers, which were hideously abundant throughout Colorado in 2010. Insectivorous Burrowing Owls sometimes share the network of burrows with the prairie-dogs and the cottontails, and these help keep the grasshopper population in check.

Peach-leaf Willow trees line the east shore of the reservoir which lies just north of the main prairie-dog colony, and a thicket of Plains Cottonwoods and other tree species at the north end of the lake provides a good source of grubs and other food types. This dense island of vegetation adjacent to water functions as an oasis in the arid grassy desert of the western Great Plains, and beckons to energy-starved migrating birds that follow the edge of the mountains as their roadway to northern destinations. The tired feathered migrants are attractive prey targets for Colorado-resident Prairie Falcons, and migrant Peregrine Falcons and accipiters such as Sharp-shinned and Cooper's Hawks.

The forest thicket adjacent to the north end of Dixon Reservoir is heavily birded in May in part because of the tremendous variety of migrants that have been found here over the years, but also because of its close proximity to the residential neighborhoods of Fort Collins and to the Colorado State University campus. Written messages summarizing accounts of the birds encountered in the forest thicket appeared on the COBirds listserve almost daily in May, and eBird checklists from Dixon Reservoir or its formal name of Pine Ridge Natural Area (named for the

Ponderosa Pine forest on the hillside to the west of the grassy valley of the prairie-dogs) were being uploaded to the eBird computers frequently as well.

In 2010, my Big Year quest required a heavy travel schedule mostly away from my local patches in Fort Collins and Loveland, and I would visit Dixon Reservoir only once during the month of May. From a local perspective, Dixon may be among the best migration traps in the Fort Collins/Loveland area, but I understood that the success of my Big Year would hinge on my ability to range far and wide throughout the state, especially during the month of May. The excellent migration traps of the southeastern corner of the state would be much more productive for adding new species to my Year List.

I would spend the first three days in May scouring these southeastern Colorado birding hot spots for off-course migrants, and I was not disappointed. On May 1st, I would add Palm Warbler and Purple Martin, both seen by Dan Maynard as well (and other birders too). On May 2nd, I added Whimbrel and Eastern Meadowlark, again in the company of Dan and others. On May 3rd, among many rarities including another Yellow-throated Warbler and another Prairie Warbler, my only new Year Bird was a Mourning Warbler seen by Dan, Alison Hilf, and Meredith Anderson at Lamar Community College.

Then early on May 6th, I successfully chased a Tricolored Heron reported from Lower Latham Reservoir in Weld County. Rushing back to my job in Fort Collins that day, a small flycatcher flew in front of my car. It was brown above, whitish below, with a pinkish color on the lower belly. This could only be a female Vermilion Flycatcher, an overshoot from southern New Mexico.

On May 7th, I added Tennessee Warbler from Lincoln County and Swainson's Warbler (Fig. 10) from Cheyenne County, both in the company of Mark Peterson. The Swainson's Warbler, an overshoot from east Texas, was found by Steve Larson of Boulder.

On May 8th, I added Gray-cheeked Thrush from Two Buttes State Wildlife Area in Baca County, and Chestnut-sided, Magnolia, Kentucky, and Black-throated Green Warblers in Lamar. On May 9th, I added Lesser Nighthawk in El Paso County, and Worm-eating Warbler in Pueblo County.

On May 14th, I returned to the migrant traps of south-eastern Colorado with Duane Nelson. I added Wood Thrush, Black-and-white and Blackburnian Warblers from Tempel Grove (Bent County) and Scarlet Tanager from Lamar Community College (Prowers County). On May 15th, I added Neotropic Cormorant from Lake Holbrook (Crowley County), Alder Flycatcher at Lamar Community College, and Blue-winged Warbler at Rocky Ford State Wildlife Area (Otero County).

On May 16th, I joined Mark Peterson and Brad Steger throughout the day. While we found numerous rare birds (e.g., Lesser Nighthawk, several Magnolia Warblers, and others), the only new Year Bird for my Big Year was a Common Black-Hawk, staked out at Fountain Creek Regional Park in El Paso County. This rare hawk from Mexico had been found by Lisa Edwards and Kara Carragher.

On May 17th, I added Scissor-tailed Flycatcher at Tempel Grove, Cape May Warbler at Thompson Ranch (Lincoln County) found the day before by Glenn Walbek, and Connecticut Warbler at Lamar Community College.

On May 21st, I added Calliope Hummingbird (very rare in spring) in Garfield County, while en route to western Colorado. May 22nd, birding with Larry Arnold around Grand Junction, I added Gambel's Quail, Gray Vireo, Pinyon Jay, Black-throated Gray Warbler, and Black-throated Sparrow. May 23rd, I added Eastern Wood-Pewee from Fort Collins' Grandview Cemetery, during a well attended field trip from the Colorado Field Ornithologists' annual convention.

The variety of birds that I observed during the peak of the spring migration during the month of May was unmatched in my experience as a birder in Colorado. I had seen an amazing 292 species in the month of May alone! My success in finding new species to add to my Year List put me on strong footing to surpass my highest previous Year List total of 370. I would end the month with 100 new Year Birds, bringing my 2010 total to 359 species for my

Big Year. I knew I could not rest now, however, because while I only needed 32 more species to match Andrew Spencer's record Colorado Big Year, I had already seen most of the expected species by the end of May. These last 32 species would not be easy. Furthermore, the abundance of rare birds discovered in Colorado in 2010 not only benefited my efforts, but also those of my competitor(s). Dan Maynard (and perhaps others) had surely had as much good fortune as I in our parallel missions to see all the birds in Colorado. I would not be able to let down my guard.

It was time to make a crucial decision. I had been able to save a little money from my job. I calculated that this financial cushion combined with some key austerity measures could sustain me for several months while I focused on my quest for the coveted 400 species threshold, never before obtained in Colorado within a single year. I gave my two-week notice at the plasma center.

CHAPTER NINE

June

I BEGAN JUNE WITH 359 species on my Colorado Big Year list. This was by far the highest Year List I had ever achieved by this time in previous years. I knew that if I maintained my momentum, that I could achieve my goal. I could break the Colorado Year List record of 391 species. I could conceivably also reach the unreachable, the coveted 400 species mark.

Of course I would need to pace myself, like a marathoner paces himself when running a twenty-six-mile race. If I work too hard at accomplishing my goal, I will run out of steam too early, deplete my scant savings account, or worse, deplete my physical and mental energy store. Yes, I could burn out, lose interest in achieving my Olympian goals. What would my parents think of me if I give up now? In my 26 years, I have never achieved an especially impressive goal that I felt my parents could feel proud of. I have not finished my college education. I have never kept a full-time job for much more than a year. I never achieved any accolades in high school academics or athletics, although I came close to getting a college scholarship in track. But close is not good enough. As my grandfather would say, "Close, but no cigar." I guess cigars were a big thing back in his day!

In reality my parents did not understand the magnitude of the feat I was attempting to accomplish. In fact, I decided to not even tell them about giving up my job just yet. This would upset them, and I figured, what they don't know can't hurt them. For a while, I avoided running into my folks, even though I lived in the same house with them. Hopefully, some day they would understand my motivations.

I wished I could compare my pace with that of the previous record holders, Mark Peterson and Andrew Spencer. These guys were my friends, and I trusted them with my life. But we all understood an unspoken rule in the competitive arena of birding: one does not boast about list achievements with other birders. I didn't want to be perceived as boasting, and I guessed that my friends would not appreciate learning of my listing success this year. Publishing list totals is ok though, and even expected in the competitive birding community.

Earlier I wrote that migration occurs at all times of the year. For terrestrial species, spring migration peaks in May but some northbound migrants continue to arrive in or pass through Colorado during the first half of June. Then, in mid-June, the migration pendulum begins its opposite swing. Southbound shorebirds and hummingbirds begin appearing in the latter half of the month, although the fall migration won't shift into high gear until mid-August.

The late arriving songbird migrants from the south are often easy to detect, as those that are males tend to sing frequently. Given the late date, they often seem somewhat desperate to attract their mate. The dawn chorus in June can be a cacophony of bird song, almost impossible to interpret with the blending of songs from so many locally breeding species. Later in the mornings, the racket of bird song recedes, but unmated males—mostly late arrivals or straggling transient migratory species—will continue advertising their positions with their unique songs for most of the day. This was the case with two Red-eyed Vireos in Fort Collins on June 7th, and another June 8th at Crow Valley Campground in Weld County.

I had traveled the fifty miles east to Crow Valley because of a vagrant Prairie Warbler that Becca Reid had photographed. I needed this off-course migrant from the meadows of the eastern USA for my Weld County Life List, which was getting close to the 300 threshold only achieved by a handful of birders. The Prairie Warbler's unique song of buzzy notes climbing up the musical scale made it easy to locate. Few other birds were singing by mid-morning when I arrived. The Red-eyed Vireo was one of these.

Becca had not noticed the vireo the day before when she observed the warbler. But her report of the rare Prairie Warbler attracted more eyes, which in turn discovered more interesting birds. In addition to the vireo, I noticed three other rare migrants at the campground: Black-billed Cuckoo, Northern Waterthrush (very rare in June), and Golden-winged Warbler. This phenomenon of one rare bird attracting the attention of additional birders who in turn find more rare birds is well known in birding circles as the Patagonia Picnic Table Effect. Its origins go back to a series of rare Mexican birds that were discovered at a small highway rest stop in Patagonia, Arizona in the last century, long before my time.

June 8th was turning into one of those special days for me, like February 16th and April 30th, with rare birds seemingly seeking me out, rather than the other way around. On my way back to Loveland, I stopped at another Pawnee National Grassland migrant trap called Norma's Grove. Here yet another rare migrant was waiting for me, a Wood Thrush. Like the Prairie Warbler, it sang incessantly. Its ethereal song was described by the late Roger Tory Peterson as the most beautiful song of America's eastern forests. Unfortunately, there probably wasn't a female Wood Thrush within five hundred miles to hear this beautiful song.

This stubborn Wood Thrush was still singing a week later when I returned to Norma's Grove with Sol Miller. No female had chanced upon the grove, but we did see a Black-billed Cuckoo, which had been found by birders as they chased the Wood Thrush. The Patagonia Picnic

Table Effect had struck again!

June is a month of intense avian nesting activity. Uncommon species that I still needed for the Big Year could be tracked down on their breeding territories, usually by listening for the male's advertising song. These mated males use their songs not to attract a female, but rather to fend off other males that may be encroaching on their territories. Some particularly defensive species, such as the Northern Mockingbird, go so far as to attack just about anything, bird or otherwise, that approaches too close to their nests.

On June 9th I joined forces again with Dan Maynard. We crossed the state to Mesa County where a staked-out Brown Pelican (Fig. 11) awaited us at Highline Lake, near the Utah border. Nearby in Garfield County we searched for a breeding pair of Scott's Oriole. The musical song of the territorial male cued us in to the right location within ten minutes of arriving at the oriole's territory in a grassy meadow dotted sparsely with ancient Utah Juniper trees.

On June 19th I used the same strategy in Huerfano County to locate two breeding territories of Hepatic Tanager and one of Grace's Warbler. I located additional territories of Grace's Warbler in Ponderosa Pine habitat in Archuleta County and Montezuma County. A pair of Acorn Woodpeckers was present at a site near Durango that has supported a small isolated colony of these handsome woodpeckers for more than a decade. The next day, territorial Lucy's Warbler and Summer Tanager were advertising their presence with song at Montezuma County's Yellowjacket Canyon near Cortez. The Lucy's Warbler was Year List #371. I had surpassed my own personal Colorado Year List total of 370 species.

My foray to Yellowjacket Canyon was as extreme, and risky, as any birding I had done all year. I almost did not make it out alive. Aside from the known hazards of venomous rattlesnake bites and scorpion stings, dehydration and the sheer remoteness of this arid southwest canyon presented a considerable risk. If one were to twist an ankle or break a leg while scaling the sandstone hillsides, sometimes as steep as cliffs, it could be tragic. Passersby are non-existent and cell reception is nil. Traveling alone is not recommended. Unfortunately that day I was not thinking about safe birding strategies, only how to take full advantage of my brief visit to the extreme southwest corner of the state.

Well it turned out to be a lucky day for me in Yellowjacket Canyon, not only because I found my target—Lucy's Warbler. I had driven the thirty miles west from Cortez to the dirt turnoff to the canyon. The next six miles are on a two-track that winds through sandstone bluffs and arid juniper-studded desert under control of the Bureau of Land Management. I had been here in previous years with Andrew Spencer and Nick Komar. Andrew's ancient Volvo had made the trek several times so I figured my Toyota Four-runner could manage it without difficulty. It handled the off-road conditions just fine, but as I left the canyon, I noticed I had a flat tire. I had prepared myself with plenty of water, but no food and worse, no jack for changing the tire. I hadn't seen a soul all morning, and walking the six miles to the paved road would take hours in 100-degree heat.

I decided to drive slowly on my flat even if it meant destroying my rim. Well, as I said, I was lucky that day. After a mile of driving (twenty minutes of agony for my vehicle), a ranch truck came along. The driver not only offered to help, but also was an employee for a local auto mechanic in Cortez. With his help, and a two-way trip to Cortez for tools, and some ingenuity in rigging a jack that would work for my car, I was able to get out of the canyon that day with sufficient time to cross the ever so dangerous San Juan pass (over a road that is treacherous even when not relying on a spare tire) to get to Ouray to the north, and then east to the Blue Mesa Reservoir near Gunnison.

As the sun began to set behind me over the thirty-mile long stretch of the Gunnison River now submerged below Blue Mesa Reservoir, I was speeding along U.S. Highway 50 towards Gunnison, headed home to Loveland. I spotted what looked like a loon about a quarter mile away in river where it opens into the eastern portion of the reservoir. Any loon in mid-summer is unusual in Colorado as all loon species breed well north of the state. Occasionally

Common, Pacific, and even a few Red-throated Loons have stayed back in their southern wintering areas, or have migrated only part of the way back north. These summer stragglers are usually sub-adults that are not yet old enough to breed.

I pulled the car over in a wide spot along the two-lane highway and pulled out my telescope. The loon was massive, definitely plumaged as a young bird, mostly brown above and white below. What struck me most was a massive bill. Immediately I thought about the possibility of Yellow-billed Loon. This species breeds only in Alaska and the Canadian Arctic and is exceedingly rare anywhere in the lower 48 states. On average, one will be discovered in Colorado most winters among the much more numerous, but similar in size and plumage, Common Loons.

I spent the last thirty minutes of daylight, and two hours the following morning, trying to get identifiable photographs through my telescope. With the great distance, my best photo was barely identifiable, but I received supportive comments from several birding friends such as Nick Komar, Brandon Percival, and Mark Peterson. I also sent the photos to other knowledgeable observers from the West Coast, where Yellow-billed Loon occurs a bit more frequently. Well-respected bird experts Steve Mlodinow and Paul Lehman agreed with the identification.

Like some sub-adult gulls, loons in non-breeding plumage can be extremely difficult to identify. Several other birders from western Colorado would see this loon in subsequent days, and some felt it was a Common Loon. A witness-quality photo of this loon (Fig. 12) is available for readers to draw their own conclusions. This would be the first summer record of Yellow-billed Loon in Colorado.

On the last day of June, I joined Mark Peterson and Brad Steger on their monthly Big Day. We started birding well before dawn in the foothills of Fremont County, ventured south to Huerfano County, then, reuniting with the Arkansas River valley, and finally north into Cheyenne County. We returned to our starting point in Colorado Springs (Mark's house) at about 10 p.m. While we found well over 100 species that day, only one would be new for my Colorado Big Year list—Dickcissel (#375). Two of these grassland birds were singing on breeding territories in Bent County.

CHAPTER 10

July

MY FIRST BIG YEAR BIRD in July was Rufous Hummingbird (#376). I had gone for a hike with my father at Storm Mountain a few miles west of Loveland on July 3rd. We have been hiking this mountain all my life, and all his life. We hunt here during turkey season and mule deer season. Now part of Roosevelt National Forest, Storm Mountain was originally settled by my great great-grandparents. Storm Mountain reaches an altitude above 9000 feet, and technically forms part of the foothills of the Rocky Mountains, rising just 4000 feet above the altitude of the Great Plains where the flat land meets the Rockies. The habitat here is principally Ponderosa Pine forest.

Hummingbirds are among the first species to begin their southward migration. The summer resident Broad-tailed Hummingbirds of the mountains must compete for nectar sources with an onslaught of migrating Rufous Hummingbirds, and a smaller number of Calliope Hummingbirds, beginning in the final days of June. These southward migrants breed in the Pacific Northwest, and follow the eastern edge of the Rockies back to their

Mexican wintering grounds. They are very rare as spring migrants in Colorado, preferring to migrate north along the Pacific Coast.

Birding was not my main focus on the hike. Spending time with members of my family had become a challenge, as so much of my time was now focused on canvassing the massive state of Colorado in search of new species for my Big Year. My father had invited me on this hike, and I felt obliged to honor his request. Of course I carried my binoculars, just in case an interesting bird crossed our path. Like most competitive birders, I don't think a minute goes by when I am not prepared mentally to notice an interesting bird in my path. This constant state of alertness hones our observation skills to an elevated state relative to the general population.

Indeed an unusual bird did appear—a high flying Black Swift. Black Swifts present an enigma among Colorado-breeding birds. Firstly, they are almost never seen during migration between Colorado and their wintering grounds. Thus, their migration routes and behaviors are unknown. Furthermore, their wintering grounds have not yet been discovered, although occasional Black Swifts are seen in winter in Central America.

The difficulty in finding their winter haunts stems from the fact that these swifts are not numerous to begin with. In Larimer County, only a couple of breeding locations are known for them, with just a few pairs high in

Rocky Mountain National Park. They are very particular about their breeding sites. They nest on narrow cliff ledges in caves typically behind waterfalls.

The scarcity of their breeding sites led ornithologists to believe that Black Swifts were indeed a rare species, breeding in just a few dozen locations throughout the American west. However, Colorado ornithologists Rich Levad and Kim Potter have uncovered dozens of nest sites in recent years within Colorado alone, a product of heroic efforts to reach some of the most remote waterfalls in the Rocky Mountains. Their work has been published in Levad's book *The Coolest Bird: A Natural History of the Black Swift and Those Who Have Pursued It.* Sadly, Rich developed Lou Gehrig's disease and died in 2008. With Rich's passing, Colorado lost a great contributor to its birding community.

The swift was not a new species for my Year List, as I had seen one on a nest at Box Canyon in Ouray a couple of weeks earlier. Box Canyon is the easiest place in Colorado for birders to see these swifts once they arrive for nesting in June. An eco-tourist attraction enables visitors to walk into the cave at the foot of the falls, and most tourists walk unwittingly within ten feet of the closest nests. This is a must see for any birder visiting western Colorado in the summer months.

I would add new species to my Big Year list the next day, however. Nick Komar joined me on a targeted birding trek to the northeast corner of the state. July 4th turned out to be another magical day, like Feb 16th and April 30th and June 8th. I found my one target (Northern Bobwhite, #377) easily at Tamarack Ranch State Wildlife Area, a rich riparian area along the South Platte River. We also stumbled upon numerous species, all singing, that do not normally establish breeding territories in Colorado. These included Wood Thrush (first state record for July) and Black-billed Cuckoo at Tamarack Ranch State Wildlife Area, and in the nearby town of Ovid, Carolina Wren and Pine Warbler.

These birds were probably unmated males that during their northward migration strayed too far from the other individuals of their population. Alternatively, their first nest attempt farther east or farther north may have failed, and they are now wandering to wherever the winds may take them, waiting for the daylight cues and their fat stores to induce them to turn around for their southward migration.

This phenomenon occurs with water birds too, especially young birds not yet mature enough to breed. Unlike songbirds, most of which reach breeding age by their first summer, species like gulls and loons do not breed until at least their second summer, and not until their fifth summer for some species. The summering Yellow-billed Loon at Blue Mesa Reservoir provides such an example. Another summering loon was discovered in early July by Mike Blatchley: a sub-adult Pacific Loon at McIntosh

Reservoir in Boulder County. I added this species (#378) on July 12th, in the company of Bob Zilly.

July is a month of reduced birding in Colorado, mainly because the songbird migration is quiet. Fall migration picks up steam in August, and peaks in September. By mid-July, the breeding birds are becoming quiet as well. With nesting well under way, and in many cases, finished, male songbirds sing only briefly at dawn or not at all. However, as the July 4th outing demonstrated, many interesting birds may be about. In late July, post-breeding dispersal of birds prior to fall migration was sure to bring even more interesting birds to the state.

On the last day of the month, I ventured out east, almost to the Kansas border, in search of more eastern wanderers. What I found were wanderers from the south, probably from Texas. I added a singing Inca Dove (#379) at Haxtun in Phillips County (first county record) and a subadult Laughing Gull (#380, Fig. 13) at Prewitt Reservoir in Washington County.

Plates

THE IMAGES IN THE FOLLOWING Figures and other photographs taken in 2010 during Cole Wild's Colorado Big Year may be viewed in color by visiting:

www.outskirtspress.com/wildbirdingcolorado.

Figure 2. **Snowy Owl**. Peyton, El Paso County, Colorado. 11 January 2010.

Figure 3. **White-winged Crossbill**. Grandview Cemetery, Fort Collins, Larimer County, Colorado. 5 March 2010.

Figure 4. **Long-eared Owl**. Nunn, Weld County,
Colorado. 16 February 2010.

Figure 5. **Pine Grosbeak**. Gould, Jackson County, Colorado. 13 March 2010.

Figure 6. **Northern Pygmy-Owl**. Bellvue, Larimer County, Colorado. 28 March 2010.

Figure 7. **Sage Sparrow**. Chatfield State Park, Jefferson County, Colorado. 20 March 2010.

Figure 8. **Yellow-throated Warbler**. Crow Valley Campground, Briggsdale, Weld County, Colorado. 9 April 2010.

Figure 9. **Yellow-crowned Night-Heron**. Fountain Creek Regional Park, Fountain, El Paso County, Colorado. 19 April 2010.

Figure 10. **Swainson's Warbler**. Cheyenne Ranch, Cheyenne County, Colorado. 7 May 2010.

Figure 11. **Brown Pelican**. Highline Lake State Park, Mesa County, Colorado. 9 June 2010.

Figure 12. **Yellow-billed Loon**. Blue Mesa Reservoir, Gunnison County, Colorado. 20 June 2010.

Figure 13. **Laughing Gull**. Prewitt Reservoir, Washington County, Colorado. 30 July 2010.

Figure 14. **Eastern Towhee**. La Veta, Huerfano County, Colorado. 8 November 2010.

Figure 15. **Black-legged Kittiwake**. Cherry Creek State Park, Arapahoe County, Colorado. 10 November 2010.

Figure 16. **Ross's Gull**. Cherry Creek State Park, Arapahoe County, Colorado. 23 November 2010.

CHAPTER 11

August

MUCH LIKE JULY, AUGUST RECEIVES reduced attention from birders. Southbound migrants are numerous but largely pass through unnoticed. Migrating songbirds are generally silent, and disguised in non-breeding plumage which tends to be quite drab. Large waves of shorebirds (sandpipers and allies), especially the adults which move south before the juveniles, pass through the eastern plains, often stopping at shallow farm ponds and at the muddy shores of reservoirs that have been drained for irrigating crops.

These are the dog days of summer. To escape the unbearable 100-degree heat of the plains, families flock to the high mountains for relief, or leave the state altogether for their annual vacation before schools resume in mid-August. The hot sun is bearable at high elevation (rarely exceeds 80° F above 9000 feet) but is warm enough to melt the several feet of snow that accumulated the previous spring. The shrinking glaciers of the alpine tundra supply ample water to the mountain streams that feed the roaring brooks and then the raging rivers, which relax somewhat once they meet the plains.

These swollen waterways of the lower elevations slowly replenish the reservoirs of the plains for the next irrigation season. Colorado's Rocky Mountains are the source of much of our nation's water supply, generated from the massive watersheds of the Colorado, Arkansas, Rio Grande and South Platte Rivers. Other rivers in Colorado that are less well-known include the Cache La Poudre, Big Thomson, St. Vrain, Republican, Purgatoire, Animas, Dolores, Gunnison, and Yampa Rivers, as well as Boulder, Cherry, Clear, and Fountain Creeks.

During the spring migration I had tallied most of the shorebirds, but about a half-dozen species visit Colorado exclusively during fall migration. One of these is the Buff-breasted Sandpiper. Most years a few juveniles of this species are discovered by birders at some of the larger reservoirs of the eastern plains. I would get lucky on August 2nd, birding with Sol Miller. I had offered to show Sol the summering Pacific Loon at McIntosh Reservoir in Longmont, only about twenty miles from Sol's residential neighborhood in south-west Loveland. The water was receding due to draining for renovation work on the locks of the reservoir, so the loon was easy to spot in the shrunken lake. The extensive mudflats had attracted hundreds of Killdeer, mostly migrants presumably. I spotted a shorebird across the lake that was buff-colored all over and shaped somewhat like a Killdeer.

I immediately recognized this bird as a Buff-breasted Sandpiper (#381), an exceedingly rare bird for Boulder County. The early date suggested that it was an adult. Unfortunately, after we had approached the spot on foot hoping for an identifiable photograph, I could not re-find it. Sol never did see it. Other birders who came to find it, many hoping to find a life bird, or at least a Boulder County life bird, were disappointed as it never was seen again. No other Buff-breasted Sandpiper would be reported in the state in 2010.

The new Year Birds were few and far between now. The next mega-rarity was found and reported by Duane Nelson from the southeast part of the state along the Arkansas River. He had found a juvenile white-phase Reddish Egret at the west end of John Martin Reservoir, the largest reservoir in Colorado. This location required several miles of driving on rugged, two-track "roads." Because of its remoteness, it is birded by just one person on a regular basis—Duane himself.

Duane Nelson is a well-known extreme-birder in Colorado. He has seen more bird species in Colorado than anyone else—464 species. He is employed as a contractor for the Colorado Division of Wildlife. His job is to monitor and protect the endangered breeding populations of Piping Plover and Least Tern in the state. These threatened birds nest only at a few locations on sandy shorelines of reservoirs in the Arkansas River Valley, and Duane single-handedly ensures these birds' survival each summer by erecting enclosures to keep marauding sportsmen on four-wheelers, overzealous birders, and oblivious cattle away from the exposed and highly vulnerable nests.

Because of his location in the southeastern part of the state (he lives in a small town in Bent County), and his vocation in remote habitats, Duane has found more new additions to the Colorado State Checklist than any other active birder. His finds are typically vagrants from Texas or Mexico, and have included Royal Tern, Black Skimmer, and Sulphur-bellied Flycatcher. Duane had heard about my Big Year and was eager to help.

On August 18th, Duane took me to the location of the Reddish Egret (#382) and I observed its typical dance-like style of hunting for fish in the shallow grassy eddies of the river delta where it opens up into the reservoir. The egret pranced around with its wings held wide open, forming a shadow that enabled it to see its prey by reducing the bright reflection off the surface of the water. Other species sometimes mimic this feeding style, so we carefully observed its distinguishing features, such as dark bill and intermediate size compared to nearby smaller Black-crowned Night-Herons and larger Great Blue Herons.

No other Reddish Egrets would be found in the state in 2010, although this one apparently stayed at John Martin Reservoir for several months, evading detection by birders until October, when Duane, Nick Komar, and I would find it in the same location. More on that later.

Duane also showed me a Least Tern (#383). I had missed this species on earlier trips to the southeast in May, as they had not yet arrived. By mid-August, their breeding season was over, and Duane told me I was lucky that one tern was lingering at the reservoir. I found out later that Duane never saw another Least Tern in 2010 after that day.

The shorebird numbers at John Martin Reservoir were impressive, but the birds were very distant. I returned in the morning for better looks, and was rewarded with a Pectoral Sandpiper (#384). These are not rare in the fall— I would see many more. I rarely find them in the spring, however.

My next Year Bird would be another sandpiper, Ruddy Turnstone (#385). These are birds of rocky coastal shore-lines, and Colorado birders are lucky to find one during each spring and fall. This one was reported by Norm Erthal on the morning of August 27th from Jumbo Reservoir in extreme northeastern Colorado. Within minutes of being identified, word of the find would spread rapidly through the state by text-messaging. I received the message twice from birding friends who were rooting for me to break the Big Year record.

I read the message as soon as it registered on my iP-hone. The message could not have come at a worse time. I had agreed to join my friends Andrew and Candace

Laviolette from Fort Collins on an overnight camping trip to the mountains that morning, but when I read the news of the turnstone, I had to act fast. We were to carpool from Fort Collins a couple hours later, heading north and west. Instead I got the directions for the campsite, drove three hours east to Jumbo, found the Ruddy Turnstone scouring the pebbles along the shoreline, and drove four hours back west. I found their campsite at the North Fork Poudre Campground west of Red Feather Lakes in northern Larimer County in time for roasted marshmallows! I guess that qualifies as extreme birding. No other Ruddy Turnstone was reported in Colorado in 2010.

While hiking the next day with my friends, we flushed a Dusky Grouse (#386) from the trail. Dusky Grouse are common in the mountains, but outside of lekking season in the spring, when males strut their fanned tails and expose their colorful air sacs through their breast feathers, they can be hard to find. The best way is to hike through the sub-alpine forests until you trip on one. In the western part of the state, they are also commonly found in Quaking Aspen groves and Gambel Oak forests. This Rocky Mountain endemic grouse species was split off from the Blue Grouse complex as a separate species just a few years ago.

While hiking in Larimer County with these non-birder friends, I saw and heard at least six American Three-toed Woodpeckers. Usually somewhat scarce in the alpine forests south of Canada, their numbers in Colorado have increased dramatically in recent years because of the ample food supply caused by an infestation of pine beetles that are suffocating Colorado's montane forests. In many parts of the Colorado Rocky Mountains, the green expanse of vibrant coniferous forest is no longer evergreen, but rather a burnt orange color from the beetle larvae sucking the life out of millions of trees.

Other rare migrants encountered during the month of August included White-eyed Vireo in Larimer County August 25th (found by Brad Biggerstaff), Connecticut Warbler in Weld County August 26th (found by Rachel Hopper), Philadelphia Vireo in Weld County August 26th, and Purple Martin in Sedgwick County August 27th. None of these were Year Birds. I finished the month of August just five birds shy of Andrew Spencer's Big Year record of 391 species.

CHAPTER 12

September

SEPTEMBER, LIKE MAY, WAS A great month for migrating birds in Colorado. It seemed to me that the variety of birds turning up in Colorado in 2010 was unprecedented. Whether this owed to the increase in popularity of birding (more birders, therefore more birds found), or to the advances in communication technologies (news of rare birds spreads faster), or to environmental factors, such as global warming, was a mystery to me. Perhaps all of these factors played a role.

September birding was like a roller coaster. It was so much fun that I could not get off the ride! It started with the biggest flock of migrant songbirds I had ever encountered, on the morning of September 3rd, along the inlet canal of Prewitt Reservoir in Washington County (eastern plains). I tried to convince other Front Range birders to make the two hour trek to Prewitt to appreciate this flock, but only Glenn Walbek heeded my call. By the time he arrived from Castle Rock (south of Denver), most of the birds had vanished, although he did see some goodies that I missed.

By my count, the flock included a Red-headed Woodpecker, two Downy Woodpeckers, a Hairy Woodpecker, four Northern Flickers, three Western Wood-Pewees, a Least Flycatcher, two Eastern Kingbirds, a Plumbeous Vireo, a Cassin's Vireo, ten Warbling Vireos, a Philadelphia Vireo, four Blue Jays, a Red-breasted Nuthatch, a Pygmy Nuthatch (very rare away from the mountains), eight House Wrens, two Blue-gray Gnatcatchers, a Townsend's Solitaire, six American Robins, an Orange-crowned Warbler, a Yellow Warbler, two "Myrtle" Yellow-rumped Warblers, a Black-throated Green Warbler, three Townsend's Warblers, a Black-and-white Warbler, two American Redstarts, an Ovenbird, a Mourning Warbler, about forty Common Yellowthroats, about eighty Wilson's Warblers, a Canada Warbler (#387), eighteen Chipping Sparrows, a Song Sparrow, a Lincoln's Sparrow, two Bullock's Orioles, and ten American Goldfinches.

Later in the day while driving in Morgan County near Jackson Lake State Park I spotted a raptor kiting. From what I could see it was a medium sized raptor that had a white tail and long gray wings. I was fairly certain it was a White-tailed Kite, but as it would represent a first state record for Colorado, I would have to document it with photographs. In my rear view mirror I noticed a car extremely close to me, so I couldn't just stop. I drove about a mile before finding a spot to turn around. Unfortunately

I was not able to re-find the bird anywhere in the area. White-tailed Kite has been seen in all the states that border Colorado, so it is an expected bird to be added to the Colorado state list. Nonetheless, I felt uncomfortable identifying it conclusively with my brief view of it. If it was a White-tailed Kite, it was a mega-rarity that got away. I had a sick feeling in my stomach the rest of the day.

A few days later, the tide turned. Glenn Walbek called to inform me that he had spotted a jaeger at Cherry Creek Reservoir in the southeast suburbs of Denver. This is Glenn's local patch. Cheri Orwig and I joined Nick Komar for the ride to Denver. When we arrived, Joe Roller and Steve Stachowiak were already there. The jaeger was circling the reservoir. On one of its rounds, it flew directly overhead, almost too close for our cameras. The photos confirmed its identity as Long-tailed Jaeger (#388). Jaegers typically migrate over the sea from their Arctic tundra breeding sites to the southern oceans, but all three jaeger species appear almost annually in the state, with observations occurring exclusively in the fall. Another fall-only "pelagic" migrant, Sabine's Gull (#389), was also present at the reservoir. (The word "pelagic" refers to the open ocean.) Many more Sabine's Gulls would pass through Colorado over the next two months.

The next day, Glenn Walbek spotted a juvenile Little Gull (#390) with a flock of ten Sabine's Gulls at Chatfield Reservoir in the southwest suburbs of Denver. I rushed to the spot and managed to get some poor photos of this tiny gull. Little Gull has been documented in the state fewer than thirty times. In North America, it breeds on the south shore of Hudson Bay in eastern Canada, wintering principally along the North Atlantic coast, with a few individuals migrating south to the Great Lakes in winter. Presumably this bird was a migration overshoot, having traveled about a thousand miles beyond the Great Lakes.

Then on the morning of September 8th, Boulder birder Lonny Frye posted to COBirds that the Boulder Bird Club field trip had just found a Prothonotary Warbler (#391) at Teller Lakes in Boulder County. I was there in a jiffy. After finding the flock of Wilson's Warblers it had been associated with, I played a recording of Prothonotary Warbler from my iPhone, not really expecting a response. A warbler would not be territorial during fall migration. Nonetheless, the bird responded by flying into a Russian Olive tree right in front of me. Not only was this beautiful golden-headed gem a Boulder County Life Bird, but it was also a Colorado State Life Bird for me, and the 40th species of warbler that I had seen in Colorado this year. More importantly it tied my Big Year list with Andrew Spencer's record!

Thanks to Glenn's help in finding the Little Gull, I had matched Mark Peterson's Big Year count of 390, and then thanks to Lonny for quickly spreading word about the Prothonotary Warbler, I was able to tie Andrew Spencer's record of 391 species. I would have the pleasure of breaking the record with a bird I found myself on September 19th: Red Phalarope (#392), picking insects off the surface of Luna Reservoir in southern Weld County. I cannot describe the feeling I experienced at that moment. This odd shorebird is rarely seen on any shore, but rather, it is a pelagic species, occurring with jaegers and Sabine's Gulls far out at sea. In Colorado, it occurs almost annually in the fall. I reported this rarity to COBirds from my iPhone. I heard later that Tim Smart of Broomfield was able to get over there and see it.

I had broken the record, but the roller-coaster ride was not yet over. Fall migration was hot and heavy, and I hoped for more unexpected rarities to be discovered. Later in the year I would still have the chance to add even more winter species to my list. I felt that reaching the 400 species mark was within reach.

September 22nd was a rainy day and I anticipated that the overcast conditions might have grounded some interesting late-September migrants. At Black Hollow Reservoir in Weld County I spotted yet another pelagic fall migrant, Arctic Tern (#393). Towards the end of the day, my cell phone buzzed. A text message indicated that a possible Ruby-throated Hummingbird was visiting Bill Schmoker's feeder in Longmont. I picked up Nick Komar on my way to Longmont. We met Bill at his house with about thirty minutes left of overcast daylight. The female-type hummingbird made a silent appearance at Bill's hummingbird garden and then posed briefly in a nearby tree. The lack of buff on the underparts ruled out Broad-tailed Hummingbird, and the short bill with green crown ruled out Black-chinned Hummingbird. Bill's excellent photos would corroborate the identity as a Ruby-throated Hummingbird (#394).

By the end of September, the migration of colorful songbirds (warblers, tanagers, orioles, buntings, gros-beaks, etc.) had dissipated considerably. The weather was turning colder. The powerful screeching from large flocks of migrating Sandhill Cranes could be heard high over-head, almost too high to see. Their obnoxious flight call sounds like a car engine trying to turn over, but louder. It was time to turn my attention to the rare and striking-ly similar *Ammodramus* sparrows of the Central Plains: LeConte's, Henslow's, Baird's, and Nelson's Sparrows.

Coincident with these would be another bird of the Central Plains, Sprague's Pipit, and possibly also Smith's Longspur. These species are notoriously hard to find in Colorado, but probably overlooked by Colorado birders due to lack of familiarity with their habitats and flight calls.

Several expeditions by other birders to the grassy san-dhills near the Kansas border in search of Sprague's Pipits had been successful, suggesting that this was a good year to find one in Colorado. Sprague's Pipit is typically a soli-tary bird, drab in plumage, resembling a juvenile Horned Lark. They are more often heard than seen, and their call given in flight is distinctive—a sharp "squeet." Colorado birders had discovered in recent years that the best way to find a Sprague's Pipit in our state was to walk through a grassy knoll near the Kansas border. The pipits seemed to prefer the tops of these grassy hills, and would give their "squeet" call when flushed from the grasses.

Given the successes of pipit seekers on the eastern plains during the last week of September, Christian Nunes decided to look at similar habitats closer to home, in Boulder. Chris is a naturalist who works for Boulder County, monitoring threatened wildlife species. Some of the most vulnerable species in the populous counties of Colorado's Front Range are grassland species like Burrowing Owl, Ferruginous Hawk, Bobolink, Grasshopper and Cassin's Sparrows, and Dickcissel.

Chris knew the grasslands of Boulder County as well as anyone, if not better. He picked a grassy hilltop to look for Sprague's Pipit and, voila! He found one atop Davidson Mesa late on the afternoon of September 28th. When he re-found it the following morning, cell phones started buzzing. From Loveland, I rushed down to Boulder to the Davidson Mesa trailhead. I speed-hiked up to the top of the mesa, and together with Christian and other Boulder County birders (Bill Schmoker, David Waltman, David Alcock, Maggie Boswell, and Peter Gent) we found, and photographed, the Sprague's Pipit (#395). This roller-coaster ride just would not end.

CHAPTER 13

October

I WAS DETERMINED TO FIND the rare Ammodramus sparrows in Colorado during October. In 2008, Andrew Spencer showed me how to find these sparrows, and together we tracked down a Henslow's Sparrow and a LeConte's Sparrow near Bonny Reservoir close to the Kansas border. From many hours in the field with Andrew the year he established his Big Year record, I learned from him the key field marks to look for on these diminutive sparrows, even during the brief moments that they may be seen in flight low above the grasses and forbs. Andrew was a sponge for all information related to birding, and he knew from Nebraska and Kansas bird reports that the first two weeks of October would be the best time to look for these mouse-like sparrows.

Ammodramus sparrows, including the common Colorado-breeder Grasshopper Sparrow, are the size of mice. They are the color of the grasses and forbs in which they feed, cleverly camouflaged from potential predators such as falcons and accipiters. They are weak fliers. When flushed, they rarely rise more than six feet off the ground, or fly more than fifty feet. After landing, they deceive any observant predator by running like mice through the grasses for another 10–20 feet in random directions, making their final resting spot anyone's guess. Not only do they remain hidden from predators but also from eager birders. No wonder that they are barely known by Colorado ornithologists.

Other sparrows, such as Vesper and Savannah Sparrows (both of which are frequently misidentified as Baird's Sparrow) that commonly migrate through the grasslands of the eastern plains are superficially similar to *Ammodramus* sparrows. These sparrows behave differently, however, typically flying much longer distances when flushed, chirping loudly and frequently, and sitting up on fence wires or on low branches of small trees from which they can clearly see (and if necessary, take evasive action from) potential predators.

To find the sparrows, I headed east to the weedy prairies and grain-rich croplands of the eastern plains. I spent more hours walking through fields than one can imagine, and these efforts paid off grandly.

On October 2nd, I began the day before dawn at Prewitt Reservoir (Washington and Logan Counties), a great spot for finding interesting migrants. As the eastern horizon began to glow from the rising sun, I could hear a variety of chips and chirps high above me, emanating from night-flying songbirds getting ready to quit their southbound nocturnal migrations. I recognized some of these sounds, such as Lark Bunting (the Colorado state bird), Savannah and Lark Sparrows, and Bobolink.

To maximize one's awareness of birds, it is essential to become an auditory birder. Nick Komar tells me that he identifies 90% of the birds he observes by sound rather than by sight, especially in spring and summer. Nathan Pieplow, the editor of the birding journal Colorado Birds, is making a career analyzing and identifying bird sounds using sonograms. Andrew Spencer has invested in expensive recording equipment to document new bird sounds to science, particularly from South American species. Thousands of his and Nathan's recordings are available to the public on the Internet at www.xeno-canto.org. During May and September, the peak months of nocturnal songbird migration, Ted Floyd, editor of Birding magazine, spends more hours birding by ear at night than during daylight hours.

Auditory birding would be the key to several new Year Birds this October. The first one was Smith's Longspur (#396). I never saw the bird, but I heard its long, downslurred rattle as it migrated south over the Prewitt Reservoir dam early that morning, shortly after sunrise. A calling Sprague's Pipit was also migrating southward!

Below the dam at Prewitt Reservoir is a rich organic habitat that attracts an enormous variety of birds during migration. Massive Plains Cottonwood trees co-mingle with fruity Russian Olives, weedy and seedy fields, wet meadows, and small ponds with cattail marshes. I decided to get off the dirt road below the dam, and try to penetrate this organic jungle in search of the less obvious birds such as wrens and sparrows. I was rewarded for my efforts when a LeConte's Sparrow (#397) flushed from the dew-drenched weeds. In flight, this *Ammodramus* sparrow can be identified by a pale tail and an orange-buff rump.

With two Year Birds already registered by 10 a.m., I realized that October 2nd would be another magical day of birding in Colorado, like February 16th, April 30th, June 8th, July 4th, and September 3rd. Other rare birds below the dam at Prewitt included a Winter Wren and a Palm Warbler.

Mark Peterson had told me that he finds Sedge Wrens most years in Colorado by playing a tape of their call notes during fall migration. They will respond readily, as will Marsh Wrens. Sedge Wren migrates through the Central Plains coincident with the *Ammodramus* sparrows. I would make a point of trying to elicit responses from Sedge Wrens in wet meadows and cattail marshes of the eastern plains as much as possible to test Mark's strategy. Although the habitat below the Prewitt Reservoir dam seemed ideal for Sedge Wren, I could not find one.

However, further east in Logan County, I played the Sedge Wren call on my iPhone at a large cattail marsh below the dam at Jumbo Reservoir. Standing along the road atop the dam affords a great view of the marsh below.

Numerous Marsh Wrens responded to the recording, and then a Sedge Wren (#398) popped up and called loudly (I would find another one at Flagler State Wildlife Area in Kit Carson County the following day). A rare Golden-crowned Sparrow was also present at the edge of the marsh below the dam. Nearby at Red Lion State Wildlife Area in Logan County, I would hear yet another Sprague's Pipit flying around the top of a grassy hill.

Then at Frenchman Creek State Wildlife Area in Phillips County, I located another LeConte's Sparrow by walking through the grain-rich remnants of a cultivated sorghum field.

Nearby in the town of Haxtun, I came across a large flock of at least fifty migrants. One was a rare Palm Warbler. Another was a female finch with strong facial markings. I knew it was either a vagrant Cassin's Finch from the Rocky Mountains (more than 150 miles to the west) or a stray Purple Finch from the east (presumably central Canada). I didn't recognize its distinctive chip note as it flew off with other birds of the flock. Listening to the recordings on my iPhone I confirmed my suspicion that this calling bird was indeed the Purple Finch (#399), another testament to the importance of auditory birding. On this remarkable day in early October I had encountered four Year Birds!

I returned to Phillips County on October 5th with other sparrow seekers Roger Linfield and Joe Roller. Roger and Joe are Denver residents, but have adopted Phillips

County as their local patch. However, they both admitted that they had never birded in Phillips County in October, and were impressed with the species I had reported from three days earlier.

My friends were not disappointed. In the town of Holyoke, a large flock of warblers (including about fifty Yellow-rumped Warblers) featured several rare ones: Blackpoll, Northern Parula, Black-throated Green, and Nashville Warblers.

Returning to the sorghum field at Frenchman Creek State Wildlife Area, we flushed an *Ammodramus* sparrow with a dark tail and a dark orange rump—a Nelson's Sparrow. This was my Year Bird #400!

The weedy grasslands of the Arkansas River valley in southeastern Colorado provide more great habitat for finding rare *Ammodramus* sparrows. LeConte's Sparrows have been discovered wintering at the west end of John Martin Reservoir on various occasions in the past two decades. The receding waters of the reservoir here also create one of the best shorebird locations in the state during fall migration. Duane Nelson had reported American Golden-Plover here so Nick Komar and I made this our first destination of a two-day tour of southeast Colorado beginning October 7th. We picked up Duane at his Las Animas home at about 7 a.m., after driving almost five hours from Loveland. Duane had agreed to guide us through the rugged trails and muddy flats to reach the best viewing spots at the reservoir.

I had found an American Golden-Plover (#401) the day before at Timnath Reservoir (Larimer County), and ironically, in spite of about fifteen species of shorebirds present that day at John Martin Reservoir, we could not relocate Duane's plover. We did re-find the white-morph Reddish Egret that I had seen with Duane two months earlier in August. We presume it was the same bird, but don't really know for sure. The chances of seeing two individuals of such a rare species in Colorado in one year seem incredibly miniscule, but this year, it seemed that anything was possible.

In addition to thousands of sandpipers, hundreds of American White Pelicans, and numerous other water birds feeding and loafing in the shallow waters of the receding reservoir, land birds were also attracted to the muddy shoreline. Dozens of Horned Larks, McCown's Longspurs, and Chestnut-colored Longspurs were constantly flitting about the shoreline and calling as they would rise up and swirl overhead. Nick pointed out the call of a Smith's Longspur among them.

In trying to get close enough to the Reddish Egret for documentary photographs, we waded through thick knee-high weeds growing out of the dried mud. Numerous Savannah and Vesper Sparrows flushed nervously from the weeds ahead of us. Then a dark *Ammodramus* sparrow flushed from our feet, dipping back into the weeds just a dozen yards ahead of us. To get adequate views to identify the bird, we ran to the spot and carefully searched for it within a 30-foot radius accounting for its mouse-like evasive behavior.

After about four short flights of this camouflaged sparrow and thirty minutes of glimpsing it run away from us through the thick tall grasses, I managed to get a couple of barely identifiable photos. As we suspected, the only *Ammodramus* that would appear so uniformly dark in flight was Henslow's Sparrow (#402), and my photos would prove it. This would be the first Henslow's Sparrow ever photographed in the State of Colorado, and just the third state record. As we retreated back to our vehicle parked above the sandstone cliffs about a mile away, we continued to flush sparrows, including another *Ammodramus*, which unexpectedly sat up on a visible perch facing away from us. Its wings were drooped, exposing its dark-orange rump. We could not believe our eyes—a Nelson's Sparrow. No, this rare sparrow was not named in honor of Duane Nelson, our host for the day, but rather for Edward W. Nelson, an American naturalist active in the late 1800s, who eventually became chief of the U.S. Bureau of Biological Survey in the 1920s.

The next day, Nick and I would flush yet another *Ammodramus* sparrow at an expansive fallow short-grass pasture at Two Buttes State Wildlife Area in Baca County, near the Kansas and Oklahoma borders. In flight, this one was pale like a Savannah Sparrow. From my days studying grassland sparrows in winter in northern Mexico, I recognized it to be Baird's Sparrow (#403). It was a good birding day on the eastern plains, and we would find several other uncommon species including Yellow-bellied Sapsucker, Sprague's Pipit, Blue-headed Vireo, and Swamp Sparrow in Baca County, Broad-winged Hawk and Winter Wren in Lincoln County, and Black-throated Blue Warbler in Washington County.

My last Year Bird of the month would be Black Scoter (#404) on October 11th at Boulder Reservoir. I could thank Dan Maynard for finding and reporting this one to COBirds. I wondered if Dan was having as much fortune as I in his own Big Year quest.

CHAPTER 14

November

THE SEASONS WERE CHANGING QUICKLY with wintry weather coming on strong. Temperatures were dipping below the freezing mark every night in my home town of Loveland, Colorado. The dawn chorus was silent and walking out of my house in the mornings to feed the chickens and goats I distinctly had the impression that all the birds had flown south on the strong northerly winds.

Ah, but that was just the point. Those winds would be bringing in many more birds, although my impression that most of the land birds had already migrated south was pretty much on the mark. To find the real action, I would need to visit the lakes. The thought of rare loons, geese, scoters, and gulls whetted my birding appetite.

Wow, I had reached my record-breaking goal of 392 species in Colorado weeks ago; I had shattered all expectations by achieving the unreachable threshold of 400 species in one year just last month, and yet I still had the birding bug. I still wanted more. How far could I go? 410? 420? My reasonable target list was dwindling to well below 20 birds, but even so, anything new now would be icing on the cake, and would put my record farther beyond reach of others who might want to steal my glory.

Glory. What a concept. I hadn't felt real glory in a long time. Okay, I am young still, just 26 years old. But this kind of glory? Not since my junior year in high school, ten years earlier, when I was chasing sprinting records. Glory was what I felt when I was offered a full-ride college scholarship for track before I even started my senior year. Glory when the football coach recruited me to be the kickoff return sprinter on the varsity team, because he knew that if I could break a tackle no defender could catch me in a straight sprint. High school glory didn't last long though. My slight body was no match for the gargantuan defensemen. After several concussions I returned my football pads to the school locker room at Thompson Valley High. And a nagging foot injury kept me from breaking those sprinting records in track. My scholarship offer was revoked. Some thought I had a shot at the Olympics as a runner, but I would have to wait ten more years to achieve Olympic-level Glory.

Surely, my Olympian efforts to break the Colorado Big Year record should be worth a gold medal. Well, with about $300 left in the bank, and no employment, that imaginary gold medal would be worth the last ounces of my energy. Silver would not be good enough. And after all, Dan Maynard, my closest competitor, could be close on my heels, or even ahead of me for all I knew. So, reservoirs here I come.

My first break came on November 5th. COBirds paid off again. Josh Bruenning reported two Black Scoters and a drake Eurasian Wigeon among thousands of waterfowl at nearby Fossil Creek Reservoir just north of Loveland. I made a bee-line for the west end of the Reservoir where I spotted the Eurasian Wigeon (#405) near the close shore, and pointed it out to another chaser, Larry Griffin. This wigeon is a rare but regular stray from Siberia. The Black Scoters were apparently gone, although a Surf Scoter had appeared. Northern ducks were on the move!

Scoters breed in the high Arctic, wintering in the oceans of both Pacific and Atlantic coasts. Small numbers start their long distance migration off-course and soon find themselves thousands of miles from any ocean. Scoping the distant waterfowl on large lakes in Colorado in November can turn up these rare ocean-diving ducks, but they often don't stay long. Cheri Orwig joined me, and we checked other nearby lakes in southeast Larimer County that day. At Boyd Lake, I spotted a Red-throated Loon (#406). This loon from the marshy taiga of the Arctic coast so rarely migrates through the interior U.S. that a well-documented bird had yet to make it onto the Colorado Field Ornithologists' checklist of birds for Larimer County. I would see three more of these dainty loons elsewhere in Colorado during November. Yes, it would be a stellar month for rare stragglers from above the Arctic Circle.

There were still some land birds on my target list, and I waited eagerly for an eBird submission or a COBirds post alerting me of their presence. These targets were rare winter visitors like Varied Thrush and Gyrfalcon, and strays from other regions like Eastern Towhee (southeast USA), Long-billed Thrasher (Texas), and Lawrence's Goldfinch (Arizona). On November 7th, word came that a female Eastern Towhee was visiting Polly Neldner's productive feeder in La Veta, more than three hours away in Huerfano County, near the New Mexico border. I didn't hesitate, especially as several other interesting species had been spotted nearby at Lathrop State Park.

I left in the middle of the night, and arrived shortly after daybreak the next morning. I had visited Polly's neighborhood several times this year, and I was never disappointed with the fantastic variety of land birds attracted to her feeders. And on this warm November day I would also not be disappointed. I was looking for a plain-backed, browner version of its more common cousin, Spotted Towhee. The Eastern Towhee (#407, Fig. 14) popped into view right on cue. Even more gratifying was a small warbler that appeared near the backyard feeders, sporting a bright yellow throat and two bold white wing-bars. "Northern Parula!" I exclaimed. Parulas are never common in Colorado. They normally turn up as off-course spring migrants, overshoots from the southeast U.S. breeding grounds. This one would be a Life Bird for my gracious host, who was thrilled.

Later in the day two Red-necked Grebes and a Winter Wren made for a productive day for finding rare birds in south-central Colorado. The multiplicity of Red-necked Grebes was further evidence that water birds from the far north were migrating to and through Colorado in record numbers this fall. Like this grebe (which showed up at least four more times on my radar screen during November), and the relatively numerous Red-throated (and Pacific) Loons, Black-legged Kittiwake (a graceful gull of the oceans) would be reported in Colorado about eight times more frequently than most years. On November 10th, thanks to a call from my reliable friend, Glenn Walbek, I would add a juvenile Black-legged Kittiwake (#408, Fig. 15) from Cherry Creek Reservoir to my Big Year list.

The next day was Veteran's Day, a federal holiday. Nick Komar had the day off from work, and he suggested we tour the remote mountain lakes of North Park, a 9000-foot sagebrush prairie surrounded by 14,000-foot peaks, in north-central Colorado. As we drove west in the pre-dawn hours from Loveland and Fort Collins, rising slowly in altitude along the Poudre River Canyon, the excitement was building. Snow was predicted for North Park, one of the first storms of the season. We hoped for a bonanza of northern migrants on the pristine not-yet-frozen lakes and reservoirs of North Park.

Nick was way behind his usual pace of 320+ species

for his Colorado Year List, so we made a target list for him, with more than 20 potential Year Birds. By noon, he already had four target birds—Pine Grosbeak, Surf Scoter, and Tundra and Trumpeter Swans. It was cold—about 15° F, with light snow. Several lakes were chock full of birds. Nick openly waxed enthusiastic about his targets, some of which were my targets too—Gyrfalcon, White-winged Scoter. The way the fall was going anything seemed possible—Northern Hawk-Owl, Hoary Redpoll? There is a first for everything, right? (These would both represent first state records, if they ever could be found). Ivory Gull, Ross's Gull—why not?

Nick keeps an open mind for finding out-of-place birds, an approach to birding that has paid off in a big way for Nick over the years. "With a good imagination, you can see anything," he frequently jokes. He has discovered many great birds in his home county (Larimer), including Brant, Red-throated and Yellow-billed Loons, Brown Pelican, Kelp and Iceland Gulls, Parasitic Jaeger, Hudsonian Godwit, Red Knot, Blackburnian Warbler, Scarlet and Summer Tanagers, and the list goes on and on. We became so distracted by our fantasizing, we did not notice when we parked on a remote sagebrush-covered bluff high above MacFarlane Reservoir that the car headlights were on.

An hour later, the battery was dead. It took six hours to organize our rescue, communicating only by text messaging, as the cell phone signal was too weak for phone calls. The overcast night sky was pitch black and I couldn't feel my toes by the time the Jackson County sheriff's office could get a vehicle out to our position and recharge our battery.

I think the only new bird we observed all afternoon was a Horned Lark. Just one squeaky Horned Lark calling overhead, invisible in the white sky.

CHAPTER 15

November 19, 2010:
A Day to Remember

FRIDAY MORNING, NOVEMBER 19TH, I decided to go back to Cherry Creek Reservoir, just south of Denver. Glenn Walbek had been reporting some interesting birds there including Mew and Great Black-backed Gulls, and Pacific and Red-throated Loons. First thing that morning, a Snow Bunting was seen near the southwest shoreline. Although rare in Colorado, I had seen the species in February. My friend Joe Roller texted me to say he would be there in search of the bunting. I decided to take the hour and a half drive to join him.

When I arrived, Joe had met up with Glenn at the Lake Shore Loop promontory on the south shore. All but the Great Black-backed Gull had been relocated. Joe announced some exciting news before departing to rejoin his ailing wife at home in the Denver suburbs. He had spotted a Little Gull far out over the middle of the reservoir. Finding a Little Gull is a feather in any Colorado birder's cap. We are lucky if one Little Gull is spotted in Colorado each year. The idea of seeing a second Little Gull this year was very exciting (I had seen the first one—a juvenile at Chatfield Reservoir found by Glenn in September). As Joe said goodbye, Glenn got me on the bird.

As we watched the tiny white gull course back and forth in flight along the distant north shore, we reviewed the pertinent field-marks out loud. Clean pale gray upper wings, even paler than nearby Bonaparte's Gulls. Bonaparte's Gull is another small, tern-like gull present in Colorado in small numbers during fall and spring migration. There were about a dozen Bonaparte's Gulls actively hunting small fish near the reservoir's surface today.

Glenn pointed out that at the great distance, the wings appeared long and tapered, similar in shape to the wings of the Bonaparte's Gulls, rather than short and rounded as expected for Little Gull. Glenn noted the appearance of dark underwings, much darker than the white underwings of the Bonaparte's Gulls, although not as black as expected for an adult Little Gull, perhaps because of a younger age. There were no dark patches on the head, back and wings, so the bird had to be older than a juvenile, but perhaps not fully adult. The small gull would frequently interrupt its cruising to dip down to the surface in pursuit of prey, flashing a large white tail, almost too large for its small body, tiny head, and even tinier black bill. The tail almost seemed wedge-shaped, although the distance made the shape of the tail somewhat difficult to discern, even as we viewed our subject through our 60-power telescopes.

None of our regular gulls has a wedge-shaped tail, not even a Little Gull. I said out loud, "Have you eliminated Ross's Gull?" As I voiced this question, I knew that the oddities of the pointed wings, the gray—not black—underside of the wing, and the large, diamond-shaped tail all added up to one of the most wanted birds of North American birders—the rare and elusive Ross's Gull, a Life Bird for me and for just about every other birder I know. Glenn's jaw dropped—he knew it too. This was no Little Gull. This was indeed a Ross's Gull, an Arctic rarity from Siberia, reported only two or three times before in Colorado.

Colorado's first Ross's Gull was found by Bill and Inez Prather on April 28th, 1983, at Jumbo Reservoir near the Nebraska border. For two weeks it was seen by dozens of other Colorado birders, of whom only a few are still birding in the state today. A second Ross's Gull was spotted at a great distance by Brandon Percival and Mark Peterson at John Martin Reservoir on October 14th, 2007. Two weeks later, on October 28th, perhaps the same bird made a brief appearance at Lagerman Reservoir in Boulder County, witnessed only by Bill Schmoker. Bill is a local schoolteacher who has earned nationwide notoriety as a wildlife photographer. Unfortunately, the gull did not linger long enough to be photographed that autumn morning.

Aware of the rarity of Ross's Gull in Colorado (and anywhere south of the Arctic Ocean), we knew we needed to prove beyond any shadow of doubt that we were indeed watching a Ross's Gull frolicking afar over the fish-filled waters of Cherry Creek Reservoir.

We decided we could probably view the bird at a closer distance from the northeast shore, so we hurried to Glenn's car to drive the two miles to the northeast corner of the reservoir. As Glenn drove and simultaneously texted the news to other birders, I got Joe Roller on the phone. "Come back to the northeast corner. We think it's a Ross's Gull, not a Little Gull!" In the few minutes available for phone calls, I called several other birders that I thought might be able to break away from their Friday afternoon duties—Mark Peterson in Colorado Springs, Brandon Percival in Pueblo, Nick Komar in Fort Collins, Christian Nunes in Boulder, and Nathan Pieplow also in Boulder, among others. Glenn called Joey Kellner, who would post the breaking news to COBirds, spreading the word by email to hundreds more.

Joe Roller had not gone far. He arrived at the northeast corner as we did. We were still too far away to get photographs. We began hiking along the north shore at the base of a massive rocky embankment built by the Army Corps of Engineers decades earlier to control and store the flow of precious waters from Cherry Creek. We carried our telescopes on their tripods over our shoulders, and our binoculars and camera equipment around our necks. Joe noticed a fisherman motoring a small vessel near the shoreline and managed to charter a ride for the three of us to the center of the reservoir.

Leaving our scopes behind with some other birders who had just arrived, we waded out to the boat in the ice cold November water, holding our cameras high to avoid getting them wet. We got close enough for magnificent views of the bird flying across the bow, and then sitting on the water. We snapped hundreds of photos. At this distance, the wedge-shaped tail was unmistakable, and even the pink wash on the breast and belly was evident. Other gull species can have pinkish breasts during the breeding season, but in November, a pink breast is a tell-tale field mark for Ross's Gull. What a magnificent gull!

By now, more local Denver birders were arriving, mostly at the Lake Loop viewing spot. We retreated from our Colorado "pelagic" boat ride after about a half hour, and returned to meet the many birders arriving on the south shore. It was about 1 p.m. By 4 p.m., as the sun went down, and the birders disappeared from the shoreline, about a hundred lucky birders had responded to the news and would sleep soundly knowing that they had seen a "mega," to use a birding term. Ross's Gull is a Code 3 bird according to the American Birding Association, meaning that it is among the rarest of North American breeding birds, most wanted by all but the luckiest listers.

Over the next week, through November 25th (Thanksgiving Day), the Ross's Gull was reliably found by most birdwatchers that trekked to Cherry Creek

State Park. They trekked by the hundreds from all over Colorado, and from other states as far away as Florida and even Alaska! The gull was featured in several newspapers and on radio and television news programs. I saw it three times during that week, from as close as thirty feet away at one point (Fig. 16).

The adventure of identifying and photographing the Ross's Gull of 2010 would be a memory I will never forget. I really enjoyed having a role in helping so many others see this wonderful bird, one that topped the wanted list of so many North American birders (including my friends Nick Komar and Nathan Pieplow, who were able to see it that first afternoon). November 19th would be a very special day, indeed.

The Ross's Gull was Year Bird #409. A few days later I found a White-winged Scoter (#410) at Dry Creek Reservoir in Larimer County. I took a short break from Colorado birding over the Thanksgiving Holiday as I attended a family reunion in Nebraska. On the drive back through northeastern Colorado, I convinced my parents to make a stop at Jumbo Reservoir. Among the spectacle of some 50,000 Snow and Ross's Geese at Jumbo Reservoir (my parents were in awe at seeing so many white geese at one spot), and thousands of "white-cheeked" Canada and Cackling Geese, I managed to spot a Brant (#411), and a Black Scoter. Back in Colorado, I was broke, and ready for the home stretch.

CHAPTER 16
December

THE NUMBER OF LIKELY SPECIES to add to my Big Year list was dwindling quickly as fall ended and the barren Colorado winter set in. Gyrfalcon and Varied Thrush were two winter visitors that still seemed possible. Two permanent residents, Spotted Owl and Ruffed Grouse, would take too much effort to find in winter. A few Spotted Owls, of the southern "Mexican" subspecies, reside in remote canyons of south central and southwest Colorado, but their precise locations, if known, is kept secret because of their endangered species status. Ruffed Grouse extends its boreal distribution to the extreme northwest corner of the state at Hoy Mountain, but this location is simply too inaccessible during winter.

At this point in my Big Year, my energies (and finances) were almost completely spent. I had accomplished a Big Year list much larger than I had imagined possible. My birding Big Year was the Biggest Year ever for Colorado. I had accomplished the impossible dream, established new heights in human expectations, and expanded the horizons of the human condition. Yet I still wanted to see one or two more Year Birds.

On December 1st, Cheri Orwig and I searched for Varied Thrush and Gyrfalcon around Jackson Lake State Park in Morgan County and the Pawnee National Grassland in Weld County, on the eastern plains. It was a long-shot, and not surprisingly, we were unsuccessful. We did find some surprises however, including Glaucous-winged Gull and Long-eared Owl at Jackson Lake State Park, and Snow Bunting and a late Hermit Thrush in the Pawnee National Grasslands.

I began to look for employment, and resorted to a part-time job at Wal-Mart to keep gasoline in my tank in order to be ready to chase any new vagrants that might come along. My best hope was the Christmas Bird Counts which would begin on December 14th and continue through the New Year.

The Christmas Bird Count is an annual survey of all the birds present in a specific circle of fifteen miles in diameter, conducted by volunteer birders. In Colorado there are about thirty of these circles, with hundreds of birders participating in the counts. Circles located in populated locations like Denver and Boulder benefit from several dozen participants on the day of the survey, sometimes more than a hundred. Remote locations, like North Park, may have only a handful of observers. These surveys turn up interesting birds every year. The data generated by these surveys are accessible to the public on the National

Audubon Society website at www.audubon.org.

I typically participate in three or four of these surveys each year. My work schedule would only permit me to join one count this month, on December 17th at Bonny Reservoir near the Kansas border. I drove the four hours from Loveland with Nick Komar and Andrew Spencer (visiting from Ecuador) to join eight others at dawn at the Bonny Reservoir State Park Visitors' Center.

The eleven hardy souls had all travelled hours to arrive at the state park, because few if any birders populate the tiny, economically depressed towns of Yuma and Kit Carson Counties, in which the Bonny Reservoir Christmas Bird Count circle was located. The compiler, Glenn Walbek, divided the group into five teams to count the birds in the approximately 180 square miles of rural terrain.

I joined Dan Maynard along a five-mile stretch of the Republican River, which carries water from Bonny Reservoir east into Kansas. Andrew was assigned to count the thousands of geese and ducks on the reservoir in the center of the circle. Nick went with Kathy Mihm Dunning to the grasslands and croplands south of the reservoir. Glenn, Loch Kilpatrick, and Alison Hilf went west. Joey Kellner, Joe Roller, and Steve Larson went north. We reunited for a homemade chili lunch (courtesy of Alison) at the visitors' center.

Over lunch, we shared stories from the day's birding.

Lots of great birds had been found by all the parties. Of note was a rare Red Crossbill, several lingering migrants along the river (like Lesser Goldfinch, Brown Thrasher, and Hermit Thrush), and a Northern Saw-whet Owl being mobbed by angry Golden-crowned Kinglets. Following lunch, and a brief field-trip to see the owl which hadn't budged from its daytime roost, we all scattered back to our sectors to continue our counts.

When we reconvened after sundown to compile the final tally (and finish the chili), we discovered that we had collectively discovered 92 species in the circle, twelve more than the previous high count for that circle. Our success was testament to the unusual level of avian biodiversity present in Colorado in 2010. Unfortunately, none of the birds encountered on the Christmas Bird Count would add to my Big Year list.

I was alerted by eBird to a potential addition to the list—a Varied Thrush had been encountered in the Longmont Christmas Bird Count circle on December 17th. On Christmas Day the eBird reporter (Jane Gabrilove) gave me directions to this location near Longmont. A post on COBirds by Todd Deininger indicated that a local resident (Ken Kinyon) had seen it again that day in the same neighborhood. On December 26th, my father joined me and together we found the Varied Thrush (#412). Its loud thrush-like chip gave away its position within a loose flock of over 100 American Robins. Todd Deininger posted to

COBirds that he also found the bird later the same day. The thrush and the robins were taking advantage of the numerous berry-laden juniper shrubs and other fruiting trees in the posh, landscaped Longmont neighborhood.

I was glad to share my last conquest for my Big Year with my father. I hoped that he appreciated the unique feat that I had accomplished. My Big Year record of 412 species would be an historical accomplishment for the Colorado birding community that I hope will stand for a very long time, if not forever.

One way for my new record to be challenged in the future is for science to redefine the concept of species. The scientific community is constantly redefining species limits, adjusting the criteria for full species status of the various bird populations that occur in Colorado. For example, in 2010, the Winter Wrens that occasionally migrate through Colorado were split into two species by the American Ornithologists' Union, which now recognizes the wrens that originate in the western USA as Pacific Wren. The name Winter Wren was retained for the eastern USA birds.

The species pendulum tends to shift between lumping and splitting, and we are in an era of splitting. Thirty years ago, Baltimore and Bullock's Orioles were considered to be one species, the Northern Oriole. Eastern and Spotted Towhees were joined as the Rufous-sided Towhee. Grey-crowned, Brown-capped, and Black Rosy-Finches were just one species: Rosy Finch. Gunnison and Greater Sage-Grouse were simply Sage Grouse. Canada and Cackling Geese were all just Canada Geese. These six splits alone netted me seven additional species for my Big Year.

More species splits are on the horizon, based on scientists' improved understanding of the genetic basis of speciation. Fifty years ago, several species of juncos were thought to inhabit North America, such as Slate-colored Junco, Oregon Junco, and White-winged Junco. Then the lumpers brought them all together as one species, called the Dark-eyed Junco. Now, the splitters are considering dividing the Dark-eyed Junco complex into several species again, but possibly not the same ones as once recognized.

New divisions beyond the imagination of our predecessors are also pending. White-breasted Nuthatches, Marsh Wrens, Red Crossbills, and Fox Sparrows all may be the recipients of future identity makeovers that would expand the Colorado state list to more than 500 species.

Other new species additions to Colorado's avifauna are not due to the stroke of a scientist's pen, but rather due to the observant eyes and ears of birders. Every year we add more species to the state list. Most of the recent additions have been from the South, such as Kelp Gull, White-eared Hummingbird, Green Violetear, Broad-billed Hummingbird, Sulphur-bellied Flycatcher, Brown-crested Flycatcher, Tropical Parula, Hooded Oriole, and Streak-backed Oriole. Some have come from the North, including Slaty-backed Gull and Iceland Gull. Many more new species will find their way into the sights of the increasing number of knowledgeable Colorado birders. Our environment is constantly in flux, and this ever-changing ambience impacts our bird populations as well.

As Colorado birding enters a new decade of the 21st century, I wonder what will be the next species to grace Colorado's mountains and prairies for the first time. Likely candidates would be Black-tailed Gull from Asia, Hoary Redpoll from the North, Elegant Tern from the West, White-tailed Kite from the South, and Common Eider from the East. Finding a new species for Colorado remains one of my dreams.

CHAPTER 17

Epilogue

If one advances confidently in the direction of his dreams, and endeavors to live the life which he has imagined, he will meet with a success unexpected in common hours.

~ Henry David Thoreau

ULTIMATELY, THE BIG YEAR RECORD is not extremely important, as with any sports victory. Holding the record provides personal satisfaction for the victor. More importantly, the discoveries and observations along the road to victory provide scientific knowledge that enhances our understanding of Colorado's ever-changing bird life. What other competitive sport can make a similar claim?

Ironically, achieving greatness in the competitive sport of birding is not heralded by our society; for example, there is no birding hall of fame. In baseball or basketball, an athlete who breaks an individual achievement record is rewarded by a multimillion dollar contract. Even in the smaller, less financially endowed sports, such as Olympic swimming, gold medalists earn lucrative endorsement contracts. In birding, competition winners receive no material spoils, just personal satisfaction.

Even outside of sports, Americans who achieve new heights within their professions (e.g. architecture, linguistics, business administration, etc.) are honored by their peers with professional awards, promotions, lucrative book deals and speaker invitations, even honorary doctorate degrees. But birding? Not so. The father of American birding, John James Audubon, achieved everlasting fame posthumously (in 2010, one of his original books would sell at auction for $16 million, more than any other book ever.) In life, Audubon was a wretch, struggling to provide food for his family each day. I can relate.

Obviously, society does not value the craft of birding as it does athletic sports and established professional careers. However, the lesson provided by my Big Year achievement in 2010 is the same as any of these other endeavors. It is the same lesson that the whole world learned when Barack Obama was elected to the U.S. presidency in 2008. Obama would be the first African-American to achieve the lofty title of President, not to mention leader of the free world. The lesson is that anyone can achieve their goals, no matter how lofty, if they focus on their task and persevere. I don't think that anyone in my family, or in the birding community, would have expected me, Cole Wild, to have broken the Colorado Big Year record, but I did it!

If I deserve a Gold medal for my Big Year, then

certainly the Silver would go to Dan Maynard. Dan finished his year with 399 species. He surpassed the daunting goal of 392 species (that broke the previous Big Year record held by Andrew Spencer) and flirted with 400 species, a threshold previously thought to be unreachable in a single year in Colorado. Given Dan's rookie status in the Colorado competitive birding arena, his accomplishment was equally laudable as mine, if not more impressive.

Will my new record of 412 species be accepted in Colorado birding circles as valid? Will all my sightings be deemed legitimate? Remember, competitive birders rely on the honor system to claim new conquests. Will my reputation withstand the harsh scrutiny of Colorado's birding naysayers? One of the reasons I wrote this book is to provide the details of my journey, in part to document my achievement for myself and for posterity, but also to convince and satisfy the disbelievers among us.

In this book, I have tried to indicate who provided witness to most of my Big Year observations, at least towards the end of my marathon, when every new bird report I shared would be carefully inspected under the Colorado birders' collective magnifying glass. I have also published identifiable photographs of many of the rarer birds I managed to see, not only in this book, but also on my photography website, which readers are welcome to visit. The site can be reached from www.outskirtspress.com/wildbirdingcolorado.

EPILOGUE

I was not able to share every bird on my Big Year list with other birders, nor photograph every bird. However, there would be only fifteen species that I alone would witness on only a single occasion, without any documentary evidence. These are Bohemian Waxwing in February, Vermilion Flycatcher in April, Alder and Scissor-tailed Flycatchers, Gray-cheeked Thrush, and Blackburnian Warbler in May, Golden-winged Warbler in June, Inca Dove in July, Buff-breasted Sandpiper in August, Arctic Tern and Canada Warbler in September, American Golden Plover and Purple Finch in October, and White-winged Scoter and Brant in November. You'll just have to trust me on these!

Some species managed to evade me but they were reported in Colorado by others in 2010. These include Black Vulture, Crested Caracara, Gyrfalcon, Whooping Crane, Hudsonian Godwit, American Woodcock, Black-headed Gull, Parasitic Jaeger, Blue-throated and Magnificent Hummingbirds, Bendire's Thrasher, Phainopepla, Black-chinned Sparrow, Hooded Oriole, Painted Bunting, and Lawrence's Goldfinch.

My new Big Year record of 412 species may be an accomplishment I or anyone else will never match. But my feat should be a model for others to achieve their dreams. I too now know that I can accomplish anything I put my mind to. This book is an example. I do not yet know what lies in my future, but I don't think I will be a cart-pusher at

Wal-Mart for long. Now I know I could be the future CEO of Wal-Mart if I put my mind to it.

I finished writing the first draft of this book on December 31st, 2010. Tomorrow is not only another day, but another year, and another decade! I don't think I will be writing another book anytime soon. But I won't promise anything at this point. First things first, for 2011 I shall begin with my New Years' resolutions… Perhaps they won't come true exactly as I imagine them tonight, but I am sure that more great achievements lie ahead for me in 2011, and beyond.

Acknowledgments

SO MANY INDIVIDUALS CONTRIBUTED TO this book. First and foremost, I must recognize the contributions of my collaborator Nick Komar. Nick took all my ideas and converted them into the written word in ways that I could never have done. Writing has never been one of my strong points, but through this book project with Nick, I have learned a tremendous amount about writing, perhaps more than I have ever learned from all my high school and college writing classes put together. Thank you, Nick.

Many others assisted with the final production stages of the book. Karen and Oliver Komar provided advice and copy-editing assistance. The staff of Outskirts Press was extremely professional and helpful in the production stages of the book, including Sara Cory, and all the others who worked on the publication of the manuscript. I also thank Mark Obmascik, whose book *The Big Year* not only inspired me to attempt my own Big Year in Colorado, but also to put my story into words for the entertainment of others. Mark was kind enough to read a draft and offer helpful advice.

The entire birding community of Colorado aided and abetted my successful Big Year, the subject of this book. Hundreds of birders shared their sightings by email through the COBirds listserve (a project of the Colorado Field Ornithologists) and by their contributions to the eBird project of the Cornell Lab of Ornithology.

Many of these birders provided companionship and witness to my Big Year achievement. I value their support and encouragement immensely. To list the names of all these birders would take up too many pages, but in particular I thank (in alphabetical order) Larry Arnold, Denise Bretting, Alison Hilf, Joey Kellner, David Leatherman, Roger Linfield, Dan Maynard, Sol Miller, Duane Nelson, Cheri Orwig, Nathan Pieplow, Brad Steger, Joe Roller, and Glenn Walbek. Several individuals welcomed me into their homes during my birding outings, among them Joan and Ray Glabach of Windsor, Beverly Jensen of La Veta, Polly and Paul Neldner of La Veta, Mark Peterson of Colorado Springs, and Bill Schmoker of Longmont.

I especially appreciate five birders who shared so much of their time and experience with me during and prior to my Big Year, and from whom I learned so much: Nick Komar, Tony Leukering, Brandon Percival, Mark Peterson, and Andrew Spencer. Someday I hope to share my knowledge with others as they have with me.

I thank Chris Wood for trusting me in the capacity of regional reviewer for eBird.

ACKNOWLEDGMENTS

I thank Joseph Dunn, William Hein, and Candace Laviolette and my other non-birder friends who, in spite of my prolonged absences in their lives during my Big Year, maintained their friendships with me, and provided much needed distraction from birds and birding when I needed it most, although those distractions were few and far between.

Thanks to Grant Firl for providing the map. Data for the map were provided by the United States Census Bureau, the United States Geological Survey, the Colorado Department of Transportation, Colorado Ownership Management and Protection (COMaP) v8, and the National Oceanic and Atmospheric Administration's National Weather Service.

Finally, I must thank my family: my parents, Bruce and Ava, and my brother Cody. They put up with my unpredictable, and often irresponsible, presence in their home, and provided invaluable life support (shelter, food, etc.) not only during my Big Year, but in the years leading up to the Big Year, in which I developed my interest in birds and honed my birding skills. Also, my grandparents Gene and Beverly Wild deserve recognition for supporting my birding obsession with birding-related gifts that were critical in my development as a birder.

2010 Colorado Big Year List by Cole Wild

Format:

Birds are listed in taxonomic order following the Checklist of Colorado Birds published by the Colorado Field Ornithologists, www.cfo-link.org.

Common Name – Date and County of first sighting, Total number seen (if less than 10), P (if photographed), H (if heard only)

To view color photographs and checklists by month, please visit www.outskirtspress.com/wildbirdingcolorado

APPENDIX

1. Greater White-fronted Goose – 20Feb Logan County
2. Snow Goose – 22Jan Weld County, P
3. Ross's Goose – 20Feb Logan County
4. Brant – 28Nov Sedgwick County, 1
5. Cackling Goose – 2Jan Fremont County
6. Canada Goose – 1Jan Larimer County, P
7. Trumpeter Swan – 16Apr Lake County, 2
8. Tundra Swan – 10Apr Rio Grande County, 5, P
9. Wood Duck – 30Jan Larimer County, P
10. Gadwall – 2Jan Pueblo County, P
11. Eurasian Wigeon – 5Nov Larimer County, 1, P
12. American Wigeon – 2Jan Fremont County, P
13. Mallard – 1Jan Larimer County, P
14. Blue-winged Teal – 3Apr Prowers County
15. Cinnamon Teal – 6Mar Baca County
16. Northern Shoveler – 30Jan Larimer County, P
17. Northern Pintail – 2Jan Pueblo County
18. Green-winged Teal – 30Jan Larimer County, P
19. Canvasback – 22Jan Weld County
20. Redhead – 1Jan Larimer County
21. Ring-necked Duck – 1Jan Larimer County
22. Greater Scaup – 2Jan Pueblo County
23. Lesser Scaup – 2Jan Pueblo County
24. Surf Scoter – 16Apr Lake County, P
25. White-winged Scoter – 20Nov Larimer County, 1
26. Black Scoter – 11Oct Boulder County, 7, P
27. Long-tailed Duck – 2Jan Pueblo County
28. Bufflehead – 2Jan Pueblo County
29. Common Goldeneye – 1Jan Larimer County, P
30. Barrow's Goldeneye – 2Jan Pueblo County, P
31. Hooded Merganser – 2Jan Pueblo County, P

32. Common Merganser – 2Jan Fremont County, P
33. Red-breasted Merganser – 2Jan Pueblo County
34. Ruddy Duck – 15Feb Weld County
35. Chukar – 9Jun Mesa County, 4
36. Ring-necked Pheasant – 2Jan Fremont County, P
37. Greater Sage-Grouse – 13Mar Jackson County, P
38. Gunnison Sage-Grouse – 10Apr Saguache County, 2
39. White-tailed Ptarmigan – 28Mar Summit County, 3
40. Dusky Grouse – 28Aug Larimer County, 1
41. Sharp-tailed Grouse – 13Mar Routt County, 7
42. Greater Prairie-Chicken – 3Apr Yuma County
43. Lesser Prairie-Chicken – 2Apr Prowers County, P
44. Wild Turkey – 6Mar Otero County, P
45. Scaled Quail – 2Jan Fremont County, P
46. Gambel's Quail – 22May Mesa County, 7
47. Northern Bobwhite – 4Jul Logan County, P
48. Red-throated Loon – 5Nov Larimer County, 4
49. Pacific Loon – 12Jul Boulder County, P
50. Common Loon – 10May El Paso County
51. Yellow-billed Loon – 20Jun Gunnison County, 1, P
52. Pied-billed Grebe – 2Jan Pueblo County
53. Horned Grebe – 2Jan Pueblo County
54. Red-necked Grebe – 15Jun Jackson County, 6, P
55. Eared Grebe – 2Jan Pueblo County, P
56. Western Grebe – 2Jan Pueblo County, P
57. Clark's Grebe – 15Feb Boulder County, P
58. American White Pelican – 6Mar Kiowa County, P
59. Brown Pelican – 9Jun Mesa County, 1, P
60. Neotropic Cormorant – 15May Otero County, 3
61. Double-crested Cormorant – 2Jan Pueblo County
62. American Bittern – 9Apr Boulder County, 9

63. Least Bittern – 7Jun Larimer County, 1
64. Great Blue Heron – 2Jan Pueblo County, P
65. Great Egret – 11Apr Weld County
66. Snowy Egret – 28Apr Larimer County, P
67. Little Blue Heron – 24Apr Kiowa County, 2, P
68. Tricolored Heron – 6May Weld County, 1
69. Reddish Egret – 18Aug Bent County, 1, P
70. Cattle Egret – 24Apr Bent County
71. Green Heron – 3May Otero County, 7
72. Black-crowned Night-Heron – 31Jan Pueblo County
73. Yellow-crowned Night-Heron – 19Apr El Paso County, 2, P
74. Glossy Ibis – 28Apr Larimer County, 5
75. White-faced Ibis – 14Apr Larimer County
76. Turkey Vulture – 2Apr Baca County, P
77. Osprey – 28Mar Larimer County, P
78. Mississippi Kite – 30Apr Prowers County, P
79. Bald Eagle – 1Jan Larimer County, P
80. Northern Harrier – 1Jan Larimer County
81. Sharp-shinned Hawk – 1Jan Larimer County
82. Cooper's Hawk – 4Jan Larimer County
83. Northern Goshawk – 30Jan Larimer County, 3
84. Common Black-Hawk – 16May El Paso County, 1, P
85. Red-shouldered Hawk – 11Jan Weld County, 2, P
86. Broad-winged Hawk – 25Apr Larimer County, P
87. Swainson's Hawk – 7Apr Larimer County, P
88. Red-tailed Hawk – 1Jan Larimer County, P
89. Ferruginous Hawk – 31Jan Pueblo County
90. Rough-legged Hawk – 22Jan Broomfield County
91. Golden Eagle – 1Jan Larimer County
92. American Kestrel – 1Jan Larimer County, P
93. Merlin – 31Jan Pueblo County, P

94. Peregrine Falcon – 2Jan Fremont County, P

95. Prairie Falcon – 11Jan Larimer County

96. Black Rail – 2May Bent County, 9, H

97. Virginia Rail – 2May Bent County, P

98. Sora – 12Apr Larimer County

99. American Coot – 2Jan Pueblo County

100. Sandhill Crane – 6Mar Prowers County, P

101. Black-bellied Plover – 9May Pueblo County

102. American Golden-Plover – 6Oct Larimer County, 1

103. Snowy Plover – 24Apr Otero County, P

104. Semipalmated Plover – 24Apr Otero County

105. Piping Plover – 1May Kiowa County, 6

106. Killdeer – 6Mar Baca County, P

107. Mountain Plover – 2Apr Baca County

108. Black-necked Stilt – 19Apr Baca County

109. American Avocet – 23Mar Jefferson County

110. Spotted Sandpiper – 24Apr Prowers County, P

111. Solitary Sandpiper – 16Apr Larimer County, P

112. Greater Yellowlegs – 30Mar Larimer County

113. Willet – 30Apr Prowers County

114. Lesser Yellowlegs – 30Mar Larimer County

115. Upland Sandpiper – 24May Logan County, 9

116. Whimbrel – 2May Kiowa County, 7

117. Long-billed Curlew – 2Apr Baca County

118. Marbled Godwit – 24Apr Otero County

119. Ruddy Turnstone – 27Aug Sedgwick County, 1, P

120. Sanderling – 7May Kiowa County, P

121. Semipalmated Sandpiper – 24Apr Otero County

122. Western Sandpiper – 24Apr Otero County

123. Least Sandpiper – 24Apr Otero County, P

124. White-rumped Sandpiper – 8May Bent County, P

APPENDIX

125. Baird's Sandpiper – 24Apr Otero County, P

126. Pectoral Sandpiper – 19Aug Bent County

127. Dunlin – 24Apr Otero County, 3, P

128. Stilt Sandpiper – 7May Prowers County

129. Buff-breasted Sandpiper – 2Aug Boulder County, 1

130. Short-billed Dowitcher – 6May Weld County

131. Long-billed Dowitcher – 1Apr Larimer County

132. Wilson's Snipe – 25Mar Larimer County, P

133. Wilson's Phalarope – 24Apr Otero County

134. Red-necked Phalarope – 9May Kiowa County

135. Red Phalarope – 19Sep Weld County, 2

136. Black-legged Kittiwake – 10Nov Arapahoe County, 3, P

137. Sabine's Gull – 6Sep Arapahoe County, P

138. Bonaparte's Gull – 3Apr Prowers County

139. Little Gull – 7Sep Douglas County, 1, P

140. Ross's Gull – 19Nov Arapahoe County, 1, P

141. Laughing Gull – 31Jul Washington County, 2, P

142. Franklin's Gull – 31Mar Larimer County

143. Mew Gull – 2Jan Pueblo County, 2

144. Ring-billed Gull – 2Jan Pueblo County

145. California Gull – 2Jan Pueblo County

146. Herring Gull – 2Jan Pueblo County

147. Thayer's Gull – 2Jan Pueblo County, P

148. Iceland Gull – 16Feb Broomfield County, 6, P

149. Lesser Black-backed Gull – 2Jan Pueblo County, P

150. Glaucous-winged Gull – 22Jan Weld County, 3

151. Glaucous Gull – 16Feb Broomfield County, 7, P

152. Great Black-backed Gull – 2Jan Pueblo County, 1

153. Least Tern – 18Aug Bent County, 1, P

154. Caspian Tern – 24Apr Otero County, 2, P

155. Black Tern – 14May Kiowa County

156. Common Tern – 14May Bent County, 5

157. Arctic Tern – 22Sep Weld County, 1

158. Forster's Tern – 3May Otero County

159. Long-tailed Jaeger – 6Sep Arapahoe County, 1, P

160. Rock Pigeon – 1Jan Larimer County

161. Band-tailed Pigeon – 16May Teller County, 8

162. Eurasian Collared-Dove – 1Jan Larimer County

163. White-winged Dove – 31Jan Pueblo County

164. Mourning Dove – 29Jan Larimer County, P

165. Inca Dove – 31Jul Phillips County, 1

166. Yellow-billed Cuckoo – 7May Cheyenne County, 9

167. Black-billed Cuckoo – 8Jun Weld County, 3, P

168. Greater Roadrunner – 31Jan Pueblo County, 6, P

169. Barn Owl – 31Jan Pueblo County, 1

170. Flammulated Owl – 16May Pueblo County, 3, H

171. Western Screech-Owl – 6Mar Bent County, 6, P

172. Eastern Screech-Owl – 21Jan Larimer County

173. Great Horned Owl – 1Jan Larimer County, P

174. Snowy Owl – 11Jan El Paso County, 1, P

175. Northern Pygmy-Owl – 21Jan Larimer County, 4, P

176. Burrowing Owl – 2Apr Baca County

177. Long-eared Owl – 16Feb Weld County, P

178. Short-eared Owl – 16Feb Weld County, 4

179. Boreal Owl – 13Mar Jackson County

180. Northern Saw-whet Owl – 28Mar Larimer County, 4, H

181. Lesser Nighthawk – 9May El Paso County, 2

182. Common Nighthawk – 7May Prowers County, P

183. Common Poorwill – 16May El Paso County, H

184. Black Swift – 20Jun Ouray County, 2

185. Chimney Swift – 24Apr Prowers County, P

186. White-throated Swift – 16May El Paso County

187. Ruby-throated Hummingbird – 22Sep Boulder County, 1

188. Black-chinned Hummingbird – 3May Prowers County

189. Calliope Hummingbird – 21May Garfield County, 5

190. Broad-tailed Hummingbird – 9May Prowers County

191. Rufous Hummingbird – 3Jul Larimer County

192. Belted Kingfisher – 3Jan Larimer County

193. Lewis's Woodpecker – 7Mar Huerfano County

194. Red-headed Woodpecker – 7May Cheyenne County

195. Acorn Woodpecker – 19Jun La Plata County, 3

196. Red-bellied Woodpecker – 6Mar Baca County, P

197. Williamson's Sapsucker – 16Apr Lake County, 4

198. Yellow-bellied Sapsucker – 2Jan Fremont County, 3, P

199. Red-naped Sapsucker – 3Apr Prowers County, P

200. Ladder-backed Woodpecker – 19Apr Baca County, 7

201. Downy Woodpecker – 2Jan Pueblo County

202. Hairy Woodpecker – 2Jan Pueblo County

203. American Three-toed Woodpecker – 10Apr Custer County, P

204. Northern Flicker – 1Jan Larimer County, P

205. Olive-sided Flycatcher – 9May Prowers County, 7

206. Western Wood-Pewee – 17May Lincoln County

207. Eastern Wood-Pewee – 23May Larimer County, 2

208. Alder Flycatcher – 15May Prowers County, 2

209. Willow Flycatcher – 14May Bent County, 7, P

210. Least Flycatcher – 7May Cheyenne County

211. Hammond's Flycatcher – 7May Cheyenne County

212. Gray Flycatcher – 10May El Paso County, 6

213. Dusky Flycatcher – 7May Lincoln County

214. Cordilleran Flycatcher – 20May Larimer County, P

215. Black Phoebe – 10Apr Douglas County, 2

216. Eastern Phoebe – 2Apr Baca County, P

217. Say's Phoebe – 3Apr Prowers County

218. Vermilion Flycatcher – 6May Weld County, 1
219. Ash-throated Flycatcher – 1May Las Animas County
220. Great Crested Flycatcher – 17May Prowers County, 4
221. Cassin's Kingbird – 1May Baca County
222. Western Kingbird – 24Apr Prowers County
223. Eastern Kingbird – 2May Baca County, P
224. Scissor-tailed Flycatcher – 17May Kiowa County, 1
225. Loggerhead Shrike – 2Jan Pueblo County, P
226. Northern Shrike – 3Jan Larimer County
227. White-eyed Vireo – 30Apr Prowers County, 3, P
228. Bell's Vireo – 24May Logan County, 4
229. Gray Vireo – 22May Mesa County
230. Yellow-throated Vireo – 30Apr Kiowa County, 2
231. Plumbeous Vireo – 2May Cheyenne County
232. Cassin's Vireo – 1May Prowers County
233. Blue-headed Vireo – 2May Baca County, 4
234. Warbling Vireo – 2May Baca County
235. Philadelphia Vireo – 20May Larimer County, 4, P
236. Red-eyed Vireo – 7Jun Larimer County, 3
237. Gray Jay – 13Mar Jackson County, P
238. Steller's Jay – 3Jan Larimer County, P
239. Blue Jay – 1Jan Larimer County, P
240. Western Scrub-Jay – 1Jan Larimer County, P
241. Pinyon Jay – 22May Mesa County
242. Clark's Nutcracker – 7Mar Costilla County
243. Black-billed Magpie – 1Jan Larimer County, P
244. American Crow – 2Jan Fremont County
245. Chihuahuan Raven – 22Jan Jefferson County
246. Common Raven – 1Jan Larimer County
247. Horned Lark – 2Jan Pueblo County
248. Purple Martin – 1May Kiowa County, 7

APPENDIX

249. Tree Swallow – 10Apr Rio Grande County

250. Violet-green Swallow – 10Apr Rio Grande County

251. Northern Rough-winged Swallow – 14Apr Larimer County

252. Bank Swallow – 23Apr Larimer County, P

253. Cliff Swallow – 23Apr Larimer County

254. Barn Swallow – 2Apr Baca County , P

255. Black-capped Chickadee – 1Jan Larimer County, P

256. Mountain Chickadee – 2Jan Fremont County, P

257. Juniper Titmouse – 2Jan Fremont County, P

258. Bushtit – 2Jan Fremont County, P

259. Red-breasted Nuthatch – 2Jan Fremont County, P

260. White-breasted Nuthatch – 2Jan Fremont County, P

261. Pygmy Nuthatch – 26Feb Larimer County, P

262. Brown Creeper – 3Jan Larimer County, P

263. Rock Wren – 10Apr Fremont County

264. Canyon Wren – 2Jan Fremont County

265. Carolina Wren – 6Mar Baca County, 5, P

266. Bewick's Wren – 2Jan Fremont County

267. House Wren – 5Apr Larimer County

268. Pacific Wren – 31Jan El Paso County, 1

269. Winter Wren – 25Apr Larimer County, 6

270. Sedge Wren – 2Oct Logan County, 2

271. Marsh Wren – 6Mar Baca County

272. American Dipper – 13Mar Jackson County

273. Golden-crowned Kinglet – 3Jan Larimer County

274. Ruby-crowned Kinglet – 16Apr Lake County

275. Blue-gray Gnatcatcher – 19Apr Baca County

276. Eastern Bluebird – 20Feb Logan County

277. Western Bluebird – 2Jan Fremont County

278. Mountain Bluebird – 2Jan Fremont County

279. Townsend's Solitaire – 2Jan Fremont County

280. Veery – 17May Bent County, 3

281. Gray-cheeked Thrush – 8May Baca County, 3

282. Swainson's Thrush – 2May Baca County

283. Hermit Thrush – 24Apr Prowers County

284. Wood Thrush – 14May Bent County, 3

285. American Robin – 1Jan Larimer County, P

286. Varied Thrush – 26Dec Boulder County, 1

287. Gray Catbird – 24Apr Prowers County

288. Northern Mockingbird – 6Mar Baca County

289. Sage Thrasher – 16Feb Weld County, P

290. Brown Thrasher – 3Apr Prowers County

291. Curve-billed Thrasher – 2Jan Fremont County, P

292. European Starling – 1Jan Larimer County, P

293. American Pipit – 30Apr Kit Carson County

294. Sprague's Pipit – 29Sep Boulder County, 5, P

295. Bohemian Waxwing – 16Feb Larimer County, 1

296. Cedar Waxwing – 16Feb Larimer County, P

297. Blue-winged Warbler – 15May Otero County, 1

298. Golden-winged Warbler – 8Jun Weld County, 1

299. Tennessee Warbler – 7May Lincoln County, 2

300. Orange-crowned Warbler – 24Apr Prowers County, P

301. Nashville Warbler – 30Apr Cheyenne County, 4, P

302. Virginia's Warbler – 7May Cheyenne County

303. Lucy's Warbler – 20Jun Montezuma County, 4

304. Northern Parula – 19Apr El Paso County, 7, P

305. Yellow Warbler – 2May Baca County, P

306. Chestnut-sided Warbler – 8May Prowers County, 3, P

307. Magnolia Warbler – 8May Prowers County, 5

308. Cape May Warbler – 17May Lincoln County, 1

309. Black-throated Blue Warbler – 30Apr Cheyenne County, 3, P

310. Yellow-rumped Warbler – 2Jan Fremont County

APPENDIX

311. Black-throated Gray Warbler – 22May Mesa County, 2

312. Black-throated Green Warbler – 8May Prowers County, 5, P

313. Townsend's Warbler – 30Apr Bent County, P

314. Blackburnian Warbler – 14May Bent County, 1

315. Yellow-throated Warbler – 9Apr Weld County, 3, P

316. Grace's Warbler – 19Jun Huerfano County, 4

317. Pine Warbler – 31Jan Pueblo County, 2

318. Prairie Warbler – 30Apr Cheyenne County, 3, P

319. Palm Warbler – 1May Baca County, 5, P

320. Blackpoll Warbler – 8May Prowers County, 9, P

321. Black-and-white Warbler – 14May Bent County, 2, P

322. American Redstart – 2May Baca County, P

323. Prothonotary Warbler – 8Sep Boulder County, 1

324. Worm-eating Warbler – 9May Pueblo County, 2, P

325. Swainson's Warbler – 7May Cheyenne County, 1, P

326. Ovenbird – 7May Washington County, 6

327. Northern Waterthrush – 3May Crowley County, P

328. Kentucky Warbler – 8May Prowers County, 1

329. Connecticut Warbler – 17May Prowers County, 2

330. Mourning Warbler – 3May Prowers County, 2

331. MacGillivray's Warbler – 8May Baca County, P

332. Common Yellowthroat – 19Apr Bent County, P

333. Hooded Warbler – 30Apr Bent County, 4, P

334. Wilson's Warbler – 24Apr Prowers County

335. Canada Warbler – 3Sep Washington County, 1

336. Yellow-breasted Chat – 7May Washington County

337. Green-tailed Towhee – 1May Baca County

338. Spotted Towhee – 2Jan Fremont County, P

339. Eastern Towhee – 8Nov Huerfano County, 1, P

340. Canyon Towhee – 2Jan Fremont County, P

341. Cassin's Sparrow – 7May Prowers County, P

342. Rufous-crowned Sparrow – 6Mar Baca County, 1, P

343. American Tree Sparrow – 31Jan Pueblo County, P

344. Chipping Sparrow – 24Apr Prowers County

345. Clay-colored Sparrow – 1May Baca County, P

346. Brewer's Sparrow – 7May Washington County

347. Field Sparrow – 8May Prowers County, P

348. Vesper Sparrow – 10Apr Conejos County

349. Lark Sparrow – 24Apr Prowers County

350. Black-throated Sparrow – 22May Mesa County

351. Sage Sparrow – 20Mar Jefferson County, 6, P

352. Lark Bunting – 7May Elbert County, P

353. Savannah Sparrow – 20Mar Larimer County

354. Grasshopper Sparrow – 7May Adams County, P

355. Baird's Sparrow – 8Oct Baca County, 1

356. Henslow's Sparrow – 7Oct Bent County, 1, P

357. Le Conte's Sparrow – 2Oct Washington County, 2

358. Nelson's Sparrow – 5Oct Phillips County, 2

359. Fox Sparrow – 9Jun Mesa County, 3, P

360. Song Sparrow – 1Jan Larimer County

361. Lincoln's Sparrow – 16Apr Summit County

362. Swamp Sparrow – 2Jan Fremont County, 8

363. White-throated Sparrow – 6Mar Otero County, P

364. Harris's Sparrow – 20Feb Logan County, P

365. White-crowned Sparrow – 2Jan Fremont County

366. Golden-crowned Sparrow – 22Jan Jefferson County, 3, P

367. Dark-eyed Junco – 1Jan Larimer County, P

368. McCown's Longspur – 6Mar Baca County

369. Lapland Longspur – 16Feb Weld County

370. Smith's Longspur – 2Oct Washington County, 3, H

371. Chestnut-collared Longspur – 6Mar Baca County

372. Snow Bunting – 20Feb Logan County, 3

373. Hepatic Tanager – 19Jun Huerfano County, 3, P

374. Summer Tanager – 30Apr Prowers County, 4, P

375. Scarlet Tanager – 14May Prowers County, 1

376. Western Tanager – 10May El Paso County

377. Northern Cardinal – 31Jan Pueblo County, P

378. Rose-breasted Grosbeak – 30Apr Prowers County, 5, P

379. Black-headed Grosbeak – 7May Cheyenne County

380. Blue Grosbeak – 8May Baca County

381. Lazuli Bunting – 1May Baca County, P

382. Indigo Bunting – 24Apr Prowers County, 5

383. Dickcissel – 30Jun Bent County, P

384. Bobolink – 17May Kit Carson County, 7

385. Red-winged Blackbird – 1Jan Larimer County, P

386. Eastern Meadowlark – 2May Cheyenne County, 2

387. Western Meadowlark – 2Jan Pueblo County

388. Yellow-headed Blackbird – 16Feb Weld County, P

389. Rusty Blackbird – 3Jan Larimer County, 9

390. Brewer's Blackbird – 30Jan Larimer County

391. Common Grackle – 2Jan Fremont County

392. Great-tailed Grackle – 3Jan Larimer County, P

393. Brown-headed Cowbird – 6Mar Baca County

394. Orchard Oriole – 7May Lincoln County, P

395. Bullock's Oriole – 30Apr Bent County

396. Baltimore Oriole – 17May Bent County, P

397. Scott's Oriole – 9Jun Garfield County, 2, P

398. Gray-crowned Rosy-Finch – 30Jan Larimer County, P

399. Black Rosy-Finch – 30Jan Larimer County, P

400. Brown-capped Rosy-Finch – 7Mar Huerfano County, P

401. Pine Grosbeak – 13Mar Jackson County, P

402. Purple Finch – 2Oct Phillips County, 1

403. Cassin's Finch – 30Jan Larimer County

404. House Finch – 1Jan Larimer County

405. Red Crossbill – 16Apr Gilpin County

406. White-winged Crossbill – 3Jan Larimer County, 5, P

407. Common Redpoll – 20Feb Logan County, 2

408. Pine Siskin – 3Jan Larimer County, P

409. Lesser Goldfinch – 12Apr Larimer County

410. American Goldfinch – 2Jan Fremont County

411. Evening Grosbeak – 2Jan Fremont County, P

412. House Sparrow – 1Jan Larimer County, P

Audubon

C O L O R A D O

Connecting People to Nature

YOU can help Audubon
protect critical habitats for birds through
The Important Bird Areas (IBA)
program.
To be a part of the global effort to identify
vital areas for birds and to learn about how
YOU can engage in bird conservation and
monitoring at IBAs, please contact
Audubon Colorado or visit
http://co.audubon.org/birdcon_iba.html

Audubon Colorado
PO Box Q
105 W. Mountain Avenue
Fort Collins, CO 80524
Phone: 303-415-0130
Fax: 303-415-0125
www.auduboncolorado.org

Take your next birding adventure with

Quetzal Tours

Birding and Wildlife Observation/Photography

☐ **Expert birding guides**
☐ **Small group sizes**
☐ **Short trips**
☐ **Relaxed pace**
☐ **Birder-friendly accommodations**
☐ **Colorado Grouse/Chicken tours in April**
☐ **Programs for non-birding companions***

*(international tours only)

More info at:
www.quetzal-tours.com